Collected Thoughts

Other books by Eric James

The Double Cure (1957)
Odd Man Out? (1962)
A Life of Bishop John A. T. Robinson (1987)
Judge Not (1989)
Word Over All (1992)
The Voice Said, Cry (1994)
A Time to Speak (1997)
In Season, Out of Season (1999)
Who Is This? (2001)

Collected Thoughts

The Radio 4
Thought for the Day
Broadcasts

ERIC JAMES

continuum
LONDON • NEW YORK

CONTINUUM
The Tower Building, 11 York Road, London SE1 7NX
370 Lexington Avenue, New York NY 10017-6503

www.continuumbooks.com

First published 2002

British Library Cataloguing-in-Publication Data
A catalogue record for this book is available from the British Library.

ISBN: 0-8264-6400-9

Designed and typeset by Kenneth Burnley, Wirral, Cheshire
Printed and bound in Great Britain by Biddles Ltd, Guildford and
King's Lynn

Contents

1998

1999

2000

Preface

On Michaelmas Day this year, 29 September 2002, I hope to celebrate and give thanks for 50 years as a priest. For almost all that time I have had some involvement in broadcasting.

I was ordained to St Stephen's, Rochester Row in Westminster, where my vicar, George Reindorp – later Bishop of Guildford, then of Salisbury – was what was frequently referred to as a 'broadcast priest'. It was while I was his curate that I first helped with broadcast services.

But 50 years as a priest – and being 77 years old – has, of course, another side to it. Your doctor becomes one of your most important friends, and you do not lightly set aside his or her advice.

In August 1991, on doctor's orders, I had to give up doing *Thought* for eight months. With the encouragement of my ever-supportive producer, David Coomes, I thought a few more 'Thoughts' in May 1992. But I'm under no illusion. I suspect this book might more accurately be called *Last Thoughts* – or, at least, *Penultimate Thoughts*!

I still treasure the scripts of the first broadcast I myself devised and delivered – in February 1962, from St George's, Camberwell, in South London, where I was then vicar. That broadcast soon led to others, and particularly to involvement with a regular BBC TV programme – *Late Night Final* – when you had to comment on the main item of the news, immediately after the last news of the day was ended. Few things mark the transition to a secular society more clearly than the fact that 40 years ago it seemed quite natural to invite a parson in a dog collar to comment on TV on the day's news!

The script I most treasure was for 9 August 1962. It was holiday time, and many of the tried and tested media clergy were probably away. It was at midday that I received my summons. I was asked whether I would go to the BBC Studios at Alexandra Palace that evening and comment on an item of news – which was still coming in – that Marilyn Monroe had died. (Why it was thought that I would be an appropriate speaker on the death of Marilyn Monroe has never been revealed!) A taxi collected me at 6.30 p.m. and I was soon selecting 'stills' of Marilyn Monroe, with the producer, Peter Ferres. I remember a particularly delightful shot of Marilyn and Arthur Miller raising bubbling champagne glasses on their wedding day. Then followed a nervous light supper in the BBC canteen, an hour producing an appropriate script, and then an anxious time of waiting for the appointed hour: 11.15 p.m. That evening, two friendly young newsreaders were on duty: Richard Baker and Michael Aspel.

I remember Michael asking me – off the set – whether I had done *Late Night Final* before. When I revealed it was my first time, and that I was almost speechless with nerves, he recommended a 'thimbleful' of vodka and kindly fetched me some. I think the script for that evening may be worth reproducing:

Handover from newsreader	. . . and that brings me to the end of the News Summary and to *Late Night Final* with the Revd Eric James.
The Revd Eric James 'Still' of Marilyn with champagne glass	Good evening. I don't think many of you will need to be told who that is . . . Marilyn Monroe . . . whose death has just been in the news. I don't know about you, but I felt very sad when I first heard the news. They say she'd become a sex symbol. But she was more than that. Just listen to what she said in a recent magazine interview. 'It might be a kind of relief to be finished. It's sort of like I don't know what kind of a yard dash you're running; but then you're at the finish line and you sort of sigh – you've made it! But you never have – you have to start all over again.' And then she goes on: 'Fame to me certainly is only a temporary and a partial happiness – even for a waif, and I was brought up a waif. But fame is not really for a daily diet, that's not what fulfils you. It warms you a bit, but the warming is temporary.'

And then – one of the most tragic passages I've ever read:

'I don't mind being burdened with being glamorous and sexual. But what goes with it can be a burden. I never quite understand it – this sex symbol – I always thought cymbals were things you clash together! A sex symbol becomes a thing. I just hate to be a thing.'

Cut to Speaker | That's the kind of world we've got to, isn't it? Great big cities, factories, blocks of flats. Great big forces: East and West. Then Marilyn's world – the great world of the movies. And ourselves, often feeling like Marilyn in the great big world – dwarfed, empty – that nobody really cares.

Who killed Marilyn? I don't know. Perhaps she killed a bit of herself; perhaps the world killed her. I think every time we treat a person as a thing we are helping to build the world that killed Marilyn. Doesn't matter who it is – mother, father, sister, brother, employee, employer, girlfriend, boyfriend, pop singer, film star – we mustn't treat them as things. That's the way to kill them. They're people. God created people to be treated as people, not as things. To him, you and I are people. George, Mary, Marilyn, Colin, Martin. We're all his people.

Then I was faded out and a cross filled the screen, and I said three short prayers, ending: 'Lord, teach us to love.'

Forty years on, I don't think there's much in that programme I'd want to change. But the world has changed; and the Church is no longer given that kind of opportunity to comment on the news - except in programmes like *Thought for the Day*. And now that opportunity is 2 minutes 45 seconds, and shared – quite rightly – with people of other faiths and none. It is, I believe, as true to say that the Church has lost the opportunity it had as it is to say that the opportunity has been taken away.

It has been my experience, over 50 years in different and varied worlds – an inner city parish, a Cambridge college, an Inn of Court, and so on – that where the Gospel is intelligently, imaginatively and sincerely related to the realities of the world today, there is as genuine a response as there ever was. And, as my fiftieth anniversary of ordination approaches, I am thankful that I was myself called to be ordained and given opportunities to broadcast such as these pages reveal.

ERIC JAMES
June 2002

1

To intervene or not to intervene

Friday 10 July 1992

To intervene or not to intervene: that is often the question – for governments and individuals. The Russian economy has a huge budget deficit. Shall the West intervene? If so, how? Iraq refuses the United Nations entry to a Ministry of Agriculture building. Shall the United Nations take it lying down or intervene with vigour?

Fifty nations have been meeting in Helsinki to work out ways of peace keeping in Europe, using, if possible, the forces of NATO. It's not just an abstract question. Bosnia and Sarajevo have been on their agenda from the beginning, but almost any way of intervening will involve the possibility of getting hurt.

What more powers to intervene should the Bank of England have if and when it suspects another bank of fraud? Should the government intervene to prevent tobacco firms from advertising? When an individual is in dire poverty, should the government intervene? And how does it reach those most in need?

To intervene or not to intervene. It's not only a question for governments and individuals: it's the question at the very heart of a great deal of theology. Was God – in Christ – intervening in the world in a particular sort of way? St Paul says 'God was – in Christ – reconciling the world to himself.'

I once heard that great Bishop of Singapore, Leonard Wilson, who was imprisoned there in the Second World War, say that in the story of the crucifixion of Jesus there are minor characters who, you can say, represent two types of humanity. One man, when he heard Jesus crying out from the cross, 'ran and fetched a sponge'. Others said 'Let be; let us see.' There are those who are always 'up and doing', who simply can't be doing with doing nothing. They're the interveners. But the others are the more passive sort who'd rather not get involved: would rather not intervene, if they can possibly keep out.

But then, Leonard Wilson said, our eyes go to the central character of Jesus on the cross. We call what happened to him not the action or the intervention but the Passion. It's what he suffered that we remember. And yet he wouldn't have suffered if he hadn't done certain things or said certain things: if he hadn't intervened in this way or that when he saw someone who needed healing on the sabbath – or a woman who'd committed adultery being stoned.

To revise a familiar phrase: 'Necessity is the mother of intervention.' Yes, but that intervention doesn't always bring with it the wisdom and skill that needs to accompany it. Nor does it necessarily bring with it that love and compassion which was the very heart of Jesus' intervention.

———— •◆• ————

2

The voice of the victim

Friday 17 July 1992

In my job as 'Preacher to Gray's Inn', I preach all the sermons that are delivered there each year, except one: the Mulligan Sermon. Some years ago a judge, James Mulligan, left a sum of money for a sermon to be preached each year on the Good Samaritan. Last year, Cardinal Hume came and preached it. He was probably the first Roman Catholic to preach in Gray's Inn since the Reformation. Last Sunday we had this year's 'Mulligan' – a marvellous sermon on the Samaritan from the West Indian, Dr Sehon Goodridge, who heads up the new Simon of Cyrene Theological Institute in South London. He made the powerful point that Jesus makes you see life through the eyes of the victim, from the vantage point – or disadvantage point – of the victim, and that judges, politicians, clergy – all of us – need to hear the voice of the victims of society, and have our vision of society shaped by its victims.

I haven't been able to get that thought out of my mind all the week.

And, curiously, I've had to go back to Gray's Inn this week, because the United Nations Special Committee against Apartheid has been holding there what was called an 'International Hearing on Political Violence in South Africa'. On the first morning, I was privileged to listen to a victim if ever there was one – the Revd Dr Frank Chikane, the Secretary of the South African Council of Churches.

Dr Chikane was ordained in 1980 but was arrested and charged with treason in 1985. He was released after three months, went into hiding, and escaped to Europe, returning to South Africa in 1987, when he was appointed Secretary of the Council of Churches.

Here are a few sentences of Frank Chikane's own account of his torture, about six years ago:

> My torture involved being forced to remain in certain contorted positions for many hours until the body gave in. Once I was hung head down with my hands and feet over a wooden stick, and assaulted. The last ordeal of my six weeks involved being kept standing in one spot for 50 hours without sleep. I was interrogated and assaulted continuously by teams of interrogators who changed shifts every eight hours. My torturers asked me to make a choice between dying slowly in a painful way and collaborating with them against those I am called to minister to. At one stage they suggested that I should commit suicide to speed up my death. It was during this ordeal that I tried to make sense of the Gospel and the sermons I preached about 'loving your enemies'. One thing that kept me strong and made me survive was the experience of the Lord Jesus Christ.

Well, as the Mulligan preacher said last week: 'Jesus makes you see life through the eyes of the victim.' Most victims in Britain are not in such dramatic circumstances as Frank Chikane was; but I think it's true, nevertheless, that it's through the eyes of the victims that you get a new vision of society – if you want one.

3

The Eleventh Commandment

Friday 24 July 1992

If the private lives of all the Cabinet and the new Shadow Cabinet were known, the gutter press would have a field day, as they would if that were the case with clerics like me. 'Thou shalt not be found out' is the Eleventh Commandment. Which means there's a lucrative, tempting income for the muck-raker.

As a priest, I hear confessions. It would be the simplest thing in the world to tell the secrets entrusted to me – and despicable. But a lay person – and the press – may sometimes have an even more difficult task: to decide when it's their duty to tell.

We have confidence in a person who keeps 'confidences'. But cheap betrayal of confidences is as common as is the dark side of our humanity. So – as I say – newspapers can thrive on muck-raking.

They wouldn't thrive but for another aspect of our dark side: the side that, for one reason or another – which the Prayer Book lists as 'pride, vain-glory, hypocrisy, envy, hatred, malice and all uncharitableness' – leads us to gloat over the failures of others. Sometimes if you can lower someone else you get the feeling – the false feeling – of raising yourself. People can waste hours of precious life exulting over the faults of others. It's rather like concentrating on the contents of what we used to call a 'privy'. Reading some of our papers is much like doing just that.

Every human being is at one and the same time glorious and ghastly. We have need of law to control our ghastliness – otherwise it can savage the lives of others. Law can be too restrictive, but there's no doubt of our need of it – to protect the vulnerable and the innocent. The cry of 'Freedom' is always a good but a dangerous cry. Freedom for the pike is death to the minnow. It's the pikes – the big people – whom the muck-rakers are really after: the archbishops and cabinet ministers. There's not much money in minnows and tiddlers. Those in positions of power and responsibility – the pikes – have chosen to be where they are, or have accepted their responsibility. And if they fall from a great height, they must expect their fall to be great. Yes; but little people play their part in creating big people –

stars, idols, heroes. And we who play our part in creating such figures – who, let's face it, we need – have also to play our part in both holding them to their responsibilities and being merciful to them. Pikes need mercy as much as minnows. But the cost of mercy is never cheap. It doesn't simply gloss over. It doesn't say 'Carry on! Anything goes!' It costs more to maintain 'the good society' than that.

4

The solution

Friday 31 July 1992

Today, I've got to get the packing done – as I expect a good many of you have. Tomorrow I fly to South Africa for a month. In a way it will be a holiday, for I've nothing in my diary: no sermons, no broadcasts. And if I have any Thoughts for the Day I shall try to keep them to myself, for it's twenty years since I was last in that complex country, and my main aim will be to listen to people of very different shades of opinion, and to learn. I shall keep a diary, or rather a journal. I always do that when I'm journeying in foreign parts. It's my form of camera.

I'm going with considerable foreboding and anxiety, of course, as a general strike is due to begin the day after I arrive; and God knows what that could lead to.

By way of preparation, I've been reading a remarkable book. It's simply called *South Africa: The Solution*. It's been a best-seller ever since it came out in South Africa in 1986. It received an astonishing welcome from all shades of opinion – black and white. It has gone through a new revision each year, and is still going on selling. I noticed that when I first caught sight of its cover and title, *South Africa: The Solution*, my spirits lifted. And I guess that a good many people in South Africa – longing for a way out of their difficulties – had their spirits lifted by at least the book's title.

Of course, there's no simple solution for South Africa's problems or for many of the huge problems that surround us at the moment; but we all need fresh supplies of hope from somewhere. In fact, that book had been sent to me by a friend of mine who had bought it in South Africa, where she'd been recovering from a cancer operation. So she's a person who has needed to have hope renewed, in more ways than one. She heads up one of the great housing agencies of the Church which tries to look after the homeless in Britain, so, in her work, she knows what it is to deal with people's hopes – and fears.

SOUTH AFRICA: THE SOLUTION!
CANCER: THE SOLUTION!
HOMELESSNESS: THE SOLUTION!

There's no simple solution for any of them. But perhaps the point of a holiday is that, ground down by the pressures of the problems of life, we are renewed in hope, so that we return ready to work again at possible solutions.

The renewal of hope doesn't in fact always depend on getting away. It was just the sight of that book's title which started the renewal of hope in me, and reading some of it increased that hope. 'The God of hope fill you' was one of St Paul's prayers. 'Whatever enlarges hope,' said Samuel Johnson, 'will also exalt courage.'

(The book is: *South Africa: The Solution*, Leon Louw and Frances Kendall, Amagi Publications (PUT) Ltd, PO Box 65, Bisho, Ciskei, PO Box 92385, Norwood, 2117, (SA Representative).)

———————•◆•———————

5

Hope

Monday 28 September 1992

I was privileged to see, recently, in Johannesburg, the production of
a new play by the great South African playwright Athol Fugard. It's
called *Playland*, and it's set in a travelling amusement park encamped
on the outskirts of a South African town. The play's a powerful
parable. The time is as important as the place. It's New Year's Eve,
1989. Two men, a young white ex-serviceman from the war against
SWAPO on the South African border, and a black night-watchman
who looks after the amusement park, meet accidentally and, as the
eighties become the nineties, confront and work through their differences, and through the nightmare of guilt which they find they
both share. They both have, for different reasons, blood on their
hands. The ex-serviceman's guilt has brought him to the point of
breakdown; but both characters, in their distress, shout out truths
which in calmer moments they would keep to themselves.

'You've got to speak up in this bloody world,' says Gideon, the
white man. 'It's the only way to put an end to all the nonsense that's
going on.'

Gideon is aware not only of his guilt but of his mortality. Like a
good many soldiers, he says he's aware of having swapped jokes with
his buddies one moment, only to be praying for them in the next. It
had been his job to throw the bodies of some of his men into a hole,
like rotten cabbages – but suddenly, he found himself realizing that
one of those cabbages was some mother's son.

So far, the story may sound fairly depressing. But it's more than
that: it's a secular story about repentance, forgiveness and reconciliation, at a time when, of course, South Africa has desperate need of
such things; but like all great plays, it's not only about one country
at one time, or about only those two people. It's a play about hope
– not naive optimism, but hope that is born of facing up to the realities of existence.

Fugard gave an address to some university students in South Africa
in 1991 when he said, 'I was on the brink of being a pessimist, but
the Fugard that is talking to you now has a hell of a lot more hope

and optimism. Not naively so. I am aware of how precarious our movement towards a new reality, a new dispensation in our society is, but I would be dishonest with you if I did not say that I am one of those people who believe that we are going to win through – in the end.'

This weekend has seen the start of the Jewish New Year. As a Christian, I have hope; but hope isn't the monopoly of Christians: you find it in the Psalms and in many a Jewish story – yes, and in plays like this play of agnostic Athol Fugard: because hope is an inexhaustible gift of God, our Creator, which I believe is available to us all.

————— ◆ —————

6

Profit without honour?

Tuesday 24 November 1992

Sometimes Jesus could be very caustic about his contemporaries. He said one day that, though they could read the signs of the weather, they could not discern the signs of the times. He used a particular word to refer to a special time when we have to make decisions that are likely to have far-reaching consequences: when a new set of possibilities is offered us which we have either to accept or refuse.

It's tempting for some people to treat the subject of arms to Iraq simply as one which could embarrass a government. Others regard it as a kind of spectator sport which is being played out in Parliament, as it was yesterday, and in the courts. But supposing we were to see it as a 'sign of the times' which we must all discern – in its moral, political and theological dimensions. That task most of us would find forbidding, perhaps beyond us; but the Archbishop of York, after the end of the Gulf War, decided that a well-researched study of the arms trade was required. He asked a body called the Council on Christian Approaches to Defence and Disarmament to undertake it. Its report was published only a short while ago. It's called *Profit Without Honour? Ethics and the Arms Trade.*

The report suggests that the effects of the arms trade in the Middle East – above all surrounding Saddam Hussein – have made this a crucial time for facing the whole truth about the trade.

Of course, there's the argument that a time of high unemployment is about the worst time to confront questions about one of the major ways a country has of earning money. But that's why the moral questions involved are so important. Most of us don't say that so long as a person does a job, the morality of what they do doesn't matter. But there are other arguments. For instance, that the money that at the moment is used on armaments ought to be used on the more profound and pressing needs of our nation and of our world.

In Roman times there was a saying, 'If you want peace, prepare for war.' It's now probably more deeply true that if you want peace you must prepare for peace. And that, too, may be very costly. But one of the preparations is to face the facts and arguments concerning the arms trade.

The Report reminds us that there was a time when the slave trade was accepted by many as inevitable and natural; and then came Wilberforce, and people like him. Could it be that behind all the commotion about arms to Iraq is really a very big subject: the ethics, the control, even the abolition of the arms trade? But if we are to see the subject that way we have to 'discern the signs of the times'.

(The report *Profit Without Honour? Ethics and the Arms Trade*, largely written by Dr Roger Williamson, can be obtained from the Council on Christian Approaches to Defence and Disarmament (CCADD), St Bride Foundation Institute, Bride Lane, London EC4Y 8EQ, 020 7583 4145, and from Church House Bookshop, 31 Great Smith Street, London SW1P 3BN, 020 7222 9011.)

———— •◆• ————

7

The Scream

Wednesday 25 November 1992

'The Scream' is a painting which almost everyone knows. The face of that harrowing, terror-ridden figure at its centre is unforgettable, even if we've never heard of the artist, the Norwegian, Edvard Munch. There's a remarkable exhibition of his work at the National Gallery at the moment, including 'The Scream', which he painted in 1893. In his diary, Munch wrote:

> I was walking along a path with two friends. The sun was setting. I felt a breath of melancholy. Suddenly the sky turned blood red. I stopped, and leant against the railing, deathly tired: looking out across flaming clouds, that hung like blood and a sword over the deep blue fjord and town. My friends walked on. I stood there, trembling with anxiety, and I felt a great infinite scream pass through nature.

Munch painted what he felt and saw and heard. The person in the picture is screaming – as well as the colours. Either as a painting, or as a print in black and white, it's not a comfortable work of art. You can't stick it up on the living-room or bedroom wall. In fact, in Munch's own handwriting, in the upper red area of the painting, was written: 'Can only have been painted by a madman.'

That painting always comes into my mind when I hear one particular verse from the prophet Isaiah:

> The Voice said 'Cry!'
> And I said: 'What shall I cry?'
> All flesh is grass . . .

There are lots of people in this world who feel at some time or other they simply must cry out loud. Sometimes, of course, they are mad. Sometimes they just cannot contain the pain and anxiety they are having to bear. Sometimes it's not their own pain that makes them cry out, but the terrible things they have to observe in the world around them: starving, homeless, or ill-treated children, perhaps.

Although sermons sometimes seem stuffy, I've always felt that a preacher is meant to cry out – at least from time to time. The voice says 'Cry!' – and you know you have to. Sometimes you have to be a voice for those who otherwise would have no voice of their own.

But alongside Munch's picture, another comes into my mind. It's of someone comfortably off – man or woman – sitting in, say, the corner of a railway carriage, reading the morning paper. It's full of tragedy; but they're simply turning the pages as though there was nothing in them worth noting.

When I came out of the Munch exhibition the other day, I found myself thankful for all those who in this world are called to scream and shriek and cry – in words or paint or music – to unstop our deaf ears.

———— •◆• ————

8

Power or influence?

Thursday 26 November 1992

Some conversations you remember like a photograph.

I can't forget how, one Ash Wednesday in the early 1970s, I had to preach in the Chapel of University College, Oxford. I was invited to dinner, before the service, and was seated next to the Master, Lord Redcliffe-Maud. A painting of one of his illustrious predecessors, Lord Beveridge, caught my eye. By chance, I had just been reading Beveridge's autobiography, called *Power and Influence* – which echoed George Washington's observation that 'Influence is not government', and that government is power. I remembered that in the first paragraphs of his book Beveridge maintained that he himself had always had influence but had seldom had power.

My conversation with Lord Redcliffe-Maud on 'Power versus influence' went to and fro all through dinner. At one point, he looked me in the eye and said with a smile, 'Which would you prefer: power or influence?' He didn't wait for me to answer, he just added: 'There's a subject for your Ash Wednesday sermon!' Well, in fact I preached the sermon I'd already prepared; but those two words kept on returning to my mind all that evening. I knew that I preferred having influence to having power – but I didn't think that was necessarily a virtue. By the right use of either power or influence, the cause of the kingdom of God on earth may be set forward.

Later that evening, Lord Redcliffe-Maud brought me a small green booklet. 'I'd rather like you to have that and read it', he said. It was the Inaugural Lecture of the Royal Statistical Society by Harold Wilson, the then Prime Minister, and consisted almost entirely of his tribute to all that Lord Beveridge had meant to him when Beveridge had taught him as a research student at Oxford. As Lord Redcliffe-Maud handed me the booklet, he said: 'That will tell you a good deal about the influence of William Beveridge.'

Well, it's 50 years, almost to the day, since the famous Beveridge Report was published, at the end of November 1942. The government of the day, in which Conservative support had been a dominant element, appointed the Liberal, Sir William Beveridge, to prepare a report on Social Insurance and Allied Services. His recommendations – with some changes – had been accepted, and they were the basis of much of the Labour Party's social welfare legislation immediately after the war. The social revolution which occurred in Britain between 1945 and 1950 owed therefore a great deal to the influence of Beveridge – which makes me think that the question 'Power or influence?' may really be the wrong way of putting it. I think William Beveridge is a lasting reminder to each of us of the power of personal influence – which is one of God's greatest gifts to us in our creation.

————— •◆• —————

9

Good out of evil

Friday 1 January 1993

President Bush has been spending the start of the New Year in Somalia.

I can remember, some years ago, seeing in the New Year in Nigeria. At midnight, all the ships' sirens sounded in Port Harcourt. We danced by the light of the moon, under the palm trees, in the warm night air. Our Nigerian hosts used plastic washing-up bowls as makeshift drums. I came indoors, exhausted, after an hour, and switched on the BBC World Service, just in time to catch the end of the Watchnight Service from Westminster Abbey, and – because Nigeria is an hour ahead of England – Big Ben striking midnight.

Today, the world over, we are all wishing one another a Happy New Year. But, since the Queen's Guildhall Speech last November, her phrase *annus horribilis* has articulated some of our anxieties, here in Britain: and now, with good reason, many people are asking: 'Will 1993 be another *annus horribilis*?' – and clearly for some it *will* be.

At the heart of most of the great religions, there's a way of looking the evil in life in the face – indeed, of turning the awful things that happen to us in life into good. In Christian terms, a way of taking the crown of thorns – which comes to us all – and turning it into a crown of glory, as Jesus did: not easily; not denying the pain and evil, or evading them; not playing 'Let's pretend it hasn't happened or isn't going to happen.' Happiness, true happiness, often depends on our plumbing some of the depths of the mystery of good and evil, and being willing to do so; and true religion should help us to do just that.

Many people who are Christians are very familiar with a phrase that comes right at the heart of the Mass – the Holy Communion: 'The same night Jesus was betrayed, he took bread and gave thanks.' At the worst time he did the best deed – just when his friends let him down. He didn't let their betrayal fester and embitter him: he took their betrayal and transformed it. So what was by any stretch of the imagination a bad day, an evil day, for him, became known through-out the ages and across most of the world as Good Friday.

So, when I say on this Friday 'Happy New Year', I don't simply mean something like 'Good luck in all that lies ahead.' I really do mean: 'Whatever way things fall out for you in 1993, may you be able to bring good out of evil. May you turn the evil into good and rob the evil of its power.'

May our New Year – whatever it contains – become for us an *annus mirabilis*, a wonderful year.

10

An example of valour

Friday 8 January 1993

The name Edmund Davies may not mean much to many people; but if you say, 'The judge who sentenced the Train Robbers', a good many will immediately say, 'Ah, yes!' And if you add, 'He presided over the inquiry into the Aberfan disaster', a good many more will say they remember. And most police officers are well aware it was Lord Edmund Davies who headed the inquiry into their pay and conditions in 1978, which recommended a very considerable pay increase, and that what was recommended then still affects what the police receive now.

The funeral of Edmund Davies took place earlier this week. He was 86 when he died. He'd been ill for a long time.

I first got to know Edmund fifteen years ago, when I became what's called 'Preacher' to Gray's Inn. There's been a Preacher there for nearly 600 years. For a time, Edmund was Dean of Chapel. It's rather a good custom they have of a layman being in charge of the Chapel and its worship. Edmund relished the job. He'd been brought up as a regular chapel-goer, in Mountain Ash in South Wales. He had as good a legal brain as any judge on the Bench, so he didn't find belief a simple matter; and often he'd invite me to tea, to talk over some matter of faith that was troubling him: some question, of medical ethics, for instance, which had a religious as well as a legal side to it.

14

I always knew he'd treat me affectionately. Sometimes he'd say with a smile, 'Preacher, I'm in need of your help.' At other times he was almost like a father addressing a son. 'Eric, boy,' he'd say – and he was twenty years older than me – 'I want to be serious with you for a few minutes.' He took what I will call his own 'spiritual life' very seriously. He would often ask me to turn our private conversation into prayer before I left. But before he let me out of the door, I would catch the glint in his eye, and he would probably share with me the latest joke he'd heard – almost invariably with a Welshman at the centre of it. I can't think of anyone who could tell a tale better.

Judges don't always get a good press these days. That pained Edmund. He was intensely concerned for what he called 'judicial quality' – on which he believed the reputation of the judiciary ultimately depends. When I asked him once what quality a judge most required, he was silent for a while, and then said, to my surprise: 'Valour.' He meant by that: courage to tread a path a judge might often prefer not to have to tread – of mercy, or severity; a path which protects a particular individual or the public – or both maybe – against the hue and cry.

Edmund Davies undoubtedly set us all an example of valour – which I'd never before associated with the task of a judge, but which is, of course, in some respects, the task of us all.

———— •◆• ————

11

Lord, have mercy

Friday 15 January 1993

Earlier this week, I had to preach at what's called the New Year Service of the City of London. It's been held in the same church, St Michael's, Cornhill, for over 70 years.

I was particularly thankful to be asked to preach, for it was as a boy of fourteen that I first went to work in the City, in September 1939. The Second World War had just begun. In those terrible war-time days, my place of work was soon destroyed by bombing. I stood one morning amid hoses, with the flames still leaping from buildings – including the place where I worked. It was in those dark days that I often went into St Michael's, Cornhill.

As I walked this week from the Underground to the church, my thoughts were, almost all, of those days: 'almost all', because the midday paper had informed me that President Bush and his staff were thought to be engaged in planning raids on military targets in Iraq; and my thoughts of the burning City of London, and of bombs on those military targets in Iraq, merged and mingled in painful confusion.

On my way to St Michael's, I passed another City church, only minutes away: St Mary, Woolnoth, where, in the war, I had heard the then Archbishop of Canterbury, William Temple, wrestle with the question of the Christian attitude to bombing. It was 1943 – exactly 50 years ago – by which time we were dropping more bombs on Germany than they on us. The Archbishop put before us the terrible dilemma of war. No one could have put it better.

'How do you stop an aggressor from killing thousands of innocent people?' he asked. 'What is the most loving thing to do – to the innocent as well as to the enemy?' 'Nothing is so wrong as to fight a war ineffectively' he said. He voiced his profound respect for the pacifist. He talked of the necessity, and the difficulty, of maintaining the right spirit: concern for justice and for mercy; for the promotion of peace; persistence in penitence, which sees that no one has clean hands, no one is wholly innocent. He talked of the importance of doing our duty – when we have seen what it is; but of how complex it is to see what *is* our duty where bombing is concerned.

I reflected, as I walked on to St Michael's, that all that Temple had said 50 years ago concerning the Second World War is still true of our involvement in the bombing of Iraq, not least the question of our guilt and responsibility through the international arms trade.

I had some time to myself in St Michael's before the service began. I remembered, thankfully, William Temple, who died in October 1944. I remembered the innocent as well as the guilty in Iraq. I remembered those who would be doing my duty for me in Iraq and concerning Iraq. But, in the end, I could find no better words than: 'LORD, HAVE MERCY'.

12

The mystery of royalty

Friday 22 January 1993

Our human need of something like a monarch is huge. Nothing else could account for all the column inches of newsprint that are expended day after day upon the royal family – and not only newsprint, but ceremonial, and buildings like Windsor Castle and, of course, Buckingham Palace; and there's the household, the staff.

But the need is complex and contradictory. Five hundred years ago, Shakespeare put the paradox into the mouth of Richard the Second:

> Throw away respect,
> Tradition, form, and ceremonious duty.
> I live with bread like you, feel want,
> Taste grief, need friends; subjected thus,
> How can you say to me I am a king?

Richard is stating the obvious: that a king, in spite of himself, has the characteristics of a commoner. Shakespeare so cleverly employs that word 'subjected' – 'subjected thus'. The king, he says, is also subject – it's a brilliant pun – he's subject to grief and need.

In these last few weeks in Britain we've been having quite a tussle with this need of ours for royals who are one of us, like us, yet, at the same time, different from us. Nowadays we spy on our royals with prurient eyes and ears, cameras and microphones – to see whether they are like us or whether they're different. And on Wednesday, in President Clinton's inauguration, his 'secular coronation', we saw the paradox being worked out in the United States. They didn't throw away 'respect, tradition, form, and ceremonious duty', yet there were several moments which underscored the theme of 'one of us', and few of us could remain unmoved by the photograph, on Wednesday, of 'Bill' Clinton, before he became President Clinton, kneeling at President Kennedy's grave.

Maybe there's not only something complex and contradictory in our need, but something significant, profound and unignorable. We humans need our symbols and signals of transcendence, our language to robe our hopes and aspirations; but the language only 'works', so to speak, if the symbols speak clearly of people like ourselves.

It's the same with priests. Most people seem to need us robed – different – from time to time: at weddings and funerals, for instance. They also need to know we're just like them. Is it because, deep down, we recognize that each one of us belongs to two worlds: we're animal and earthy and all too human, yet part of us is mysterious and transcendent? If so, the paradox lies not just with the royal family, or the President. The royals only mirror and magnify the mystery of ourselves: that two worlds meet in us all.

13

We'll gather lilacs

Friday 29 January 1993

Anniversaries are the stuff of radio and television; but somehow we've all forgotten one centenary this month – the birth of Ivor Novello. Thousands attended his funeral; and, although he died over 40 years ago, there can't be many who haven't heard and hummed 'Keep the Home Fires Burning' or a melody from one of his many musical romances.

Ivor had a genius for light music, and was a master of his craft.

Some people were pompous and condescending about his creations. Even the man to whom Ivor owed most, Eddie Marsh, Churchill's private secretary, said of him at one stage: 'He has a dangerous facililty for turning out catchy tunes, which are very pretty and great fun but are not so good as they ought to be.' Fortunately for British light music, those seedy comments fell on stony ground.

I think the phenomenon of Ivor is worth pondering – not ponderously, heaven forbid! – but because our enjoyment of Ivor Novello may say something significant not only about him but about ourselves.

There never was a simpler tune than 'Keep the Home Fires Burning'. In the First World War it spoke to millions, articulated their hopes, and, for a few seconds, put to flight their fears.

True simplicity always has something God-like about it – something Christ-like. Jesus said: 'Except you become as little children . . .'

Ivor's romances were unashamedly escapist. His world was not Bosnia but Ruritania. Yet, surely, we're not meant to spend all our days grappling with the dark, profound and tragic aspects of life. One of our basic human needs is to rest, relax and be entertained: to forget reality – for an hour, or an evening – and to return to the fray refreshed and recovered, whether the means of our restoration is Ivor Novello or Inspector Morse. God made us, not least, for fantasy and fun.

Ivor was undoubtedly a charmer. He was tall, dark and handsome, and had a profile that made his fans faint at the sight of him. Take charm like Ivor's away – and the world would lose a great deal.

Switch on the radio any day, and you're still quite likely to hear:

> We'll gather lilacs in the spring again
> And walk together down an English lane
> Until our hearts have learned to sing again.

Those lines leave us quite a way from the kingdom of God; but they're not so far from the words of Jesus, 'Consider the lilies of the field . . .' or from Isaiah's 'the desert shall blossom as the rose'. There was little agony in Ivor's garden, and few thorns to his roses. But the gift of making people think of spring at dead of winter is not to be despised on a Friday morning in January.

———◆·———

14

Vulnerable God

Tuesday 22 June 1993

If the poet John Donne were in charge of the headlines this morning, he might have written: 'Every man's illness diminishes me'. It's clear that Michael Heseltine's heart attack has sent a shock wave and a shiver through a great many people, not only people at the top, in positions of political power. The 'Tarzan' image of Michael Heseltine was one of God-like invulnerability on most occasions, but the demands of his job have clearly caught up with him, and he has the sympathy of us all.

I've been interested in recent years to see how that phrase 'God-like invulnerability' has been questioned and criticized in various quarters. So many prayers in the Prayer Book begin with the word 'Almighty'. That was undoubtedly in the past one of the primary pictures and images of God. But lately, people's most profound pictures of him seem to have changed. I take as an example a prayer of which I've become very fond in recent years, which begins:

> Vulnerable God,
> you challenge the powers that rule this world,
> through the needy, the compassionate,
> and those who are filled with longing . . .

Of course, the vulnerability of God is no new idea. No one can look at the crucifixion of Jesus as the image of God and only think of God as Almighty and invulnerable. It's as though God has been trying to teach his world for centuries that a kind of 'macho' image of him is not enough. Paradoxically, he makes his power known in the weakness of a baby in a cradle – at Bethlehem – and in a man hanging helpless on a cross.

I would have to say that I've often felt as close to God in a hospital ward as in a chapel. It's where and when vulnerability and need have to be acknowledged that we often meet God. Not that God is made known in weakness rather than in power. He's known in both – in everything.

There's a message in Michael Heseltine's illness for us all, but perhaps a special message for politicians. Sometimes, it seems politics is about power and the powerful. Well, it is; but it's also about the vulnerable. It's, of course, about providing hospitals – for all. It's about the down-trodden. It's about those who have little power to help themselves – for one reason or another – not least heart attacks. It's about the vulnerable: which at some time or other includes us all.

———◆———

15

A splendid failure

Wednesday 23 June 1993

Last week, a young student friend of mine asked me to read the manuscript of his biography, as yet unpublished, of the Liberal politician Charles Masterman, who was a close friend of Churchill, and a Cabinet Minister in Lloyd George's government, yet who most people these days have never heard of. I could hardly wait to read it, not least because I'd suggested the subject to the student, and because Charles Masterman is so neglected. He was undoubtedly what Lord Beaverbrook called him: 'a splendid failure'.

Masterman lived in the South London parish where I was at one time the vicar – a long time before I was there. He chose to live for several years in the worst block of slums in the parish. They were called 'the Albany'; he called them 'the Abyss'. But there he learnt, at first hand, what it was like to be poor. Ever after, he was a politician who could talk from experience.

When he got into Parliament and into the Cabinet, he became the man most responsible for the legislation involved in bringing in National Insurance. To him, compulsory insurance was one of the most important ways there could be of decreasing dependence on Poor Relief, and of diminishing the poverty of people like those among whom he had lived. Getting the scheme through Parliament meant, of course, lots of detailed work. It meant losing friends from other parties and learning the art of compromise. But Masterman never lost his Christian convictions and, therefore, his concern for the poor.

When he was a Cabinet Minister, he wrote a letter that might have been written now: 'Let us anyhow face realities,' he wrote, 'all the unclean ways of party politics: and get through all this mud and slush. Above all, let's not relax our eagerness to do something for the poor; all the world's agin the poor!' Masterman had married someone with a title. 'I feel', he wrote, 'that I'm not so much inclined to care, or at least to break into revolt against conditions of poverty as I come to settle down in the social order . . . Don't let's ever tolerate the cruelties and injustices of the world. Pray for the fire within: adequate to burn up the sins of the whole world.'

Well, the National Insurance Act came into being because of Masterman and people like him. But, as swiftly as he had climbed the ladder of politics, he, like many another politician, fell down it, and his life ended in tragedy.

Yet at a time of talk of unclean party politics, and when the subject of poor relief is again an important item on the national agenda, there are, I believe, few politicians more worthy of our remembrance than Charles Masterman. 'Let's not relax our eagerness to do something for the poor' he said – knowing better than most what that must involve, and the seductions on the way

———◆———

16

The significance of recognition

Thursday 24 June 1993

For the last few days I've had staying with me a black South African from Soweto, Johannesburg. Bishop Trevor Huddleston had known him since he was a child, and had invited him to be his guest at his eightieth birthday, last week.

On Saturday, I took 'Chinkie' – as he was known to his friends since childhood – down the Thames to Greenwich, on a river boat, to show him the sights of London. His camera wouldn't work, and as I'm hopeless at such things, I suggested he went over to a group of young men, most of whom had cameras with them. But I hadn't realized they were white South Africans on holiday in England, and when 'Chinkie' went and gently asked their help, they quickly said, aggressively: 'Get away.'

I contrast that sad incident of rejection with what Archbishop Desmond Tutu told us at the service to celebrate Trevor Huddleston's birth. He said that when he was only a boy of eight, his mother was working as a domestic in a hostel for black blind women. One day he was standing on the balcony of the hostel with his mother, when Father Huddleston − as he then was − walked past, in a white cassock and a big black hat. 'You could have knocked me down with a feather, young as I was,' said the Archbishop, 'when this man doffed his hat to my mother. I couldn't understand a white man doffing his hat to a black uneducated woman like my mother.'

Desmond Tutu also told us that when he was thirteen he was in hospital, for twenty months, with TB − at times at death's door − and Father Huddleston visited him once a week. 'I was a nonentity,' said Desmond Tutu. But, of course, why Trevor Huddleston visited him, and why he raised his hat to his mother, was because he knew that neither of them were nonentities: they were, to him, children of God.

Yesterday I was privileged to go to Oxford as a guest of Trevor Huddleston when he received an honorary degree from the University, which he first entered over 60 years ago. For him, it was the last event of a week of celebrations of his birthday. All sorts of people have taken the opportunity to recognize what he has done in his life, particularly for the people of black South Africa. Julius Nyerere, formerly President of Tanzania, Adelaide Tambo, the widow of Oliver Tambo, and many others, have travelled thousands of miles to give him the recognition they believe he deserves.

But in recognizing him, what they have really been doing is to make clear that the centre of his whole life's work has been to recognize the significance of others and to help them to recognize their own significance.

Trevor Huddleston's life isn't over yet − he's only 80! Yet the recognition he has received can remind us all of the significance of recognition: that we all need it, and that, in ways great and small, we can all give it − or withhold it.

17

The public and the private self

Tuesday 15 February 1994

I must be one of the luckier clergy. A few nights ago, I was taken to Covent Garden by a couple whose wedding I'd recently conducted. It was a marvellous performance of Benjamin Britten's opera, *Gloriana*, by Opera North, a fairly young company, based in Leeds. The performance was rapturously received; though, when *Gloriana* was first produced, at the time of the Coronation in 1953, the critics were very unenthusiastic, some calling it *Boriana*.

The opera is about Queen Elizabeth the First, her Court and her loves, particularly the Earl of Essex. The subject gives great scope for public celebration and pageantry. But quite the most moving moment for me was when the Queen was divested of all her royal robes, and she stood, centre stage, in a simple, shroud-like shift. We had watched while every robe and piece of regalia was removed from her, one by one, including her wig. In the end, she was a tottering, balding old lady.

I can well see that, at the time of our young Queen's Coronation, the opera was felt by some to be a bit brutal – to say the least. But in the intervening years, the conflict between the public and the private life of royalty has become a common topic of conversation; and, recently, each week has seemed to provide yet another example of conflict between the public role of, say, a politician and his or her private life: often with attendant pain and tragedy.

But why that moment in *Gloriana*, when the Queen was slowly divested before our eyes, was so moving, was, I've no doubt, because it spoke to each one of us present about ourselves. We all have a public and a private self, and none of us would care for all our private self to be exposed to public view.

Today is Shrove Tuesday; tomorrow, Ash Wednesday: the beginning of the 40 days and 40 nights we call 'Lent', which lead up to Good Friday.

It's not a bad idea to think of Lent as a time when we try to face again our private self. We should not underestimate how demanding that can sometimes be; but it helps me to remember, when I try to do that, that at the heart of the Christian religion is not some regal figure of earthly majesty and power, but one who, upon the cross, robed in our flesh – but in little else – is the very image of vulnerability.

There is, in fact, no way of closing the gap between our public and our private self that does not involve facing up to our vulnerability.

Benjamin Britten made such a good job of *Gloriana*, not least because something of himself was in his subject: the vulnerability of the artist, and the conflict of his public and private life. For most of us, it provides, at least in part, something of the way of the cross.

———— • ◆ • ————

18

Making our mark

Saturday 8 July 1995

My Thought for the Day is a kind of poem that's a prayer.

> Lord, I think you've made us
> so that each of us needs to make our mark.
> And if we can't –
> or feel we can't –
> that only makes us feel we need to make it
> all the more.
>
> The more we feel we haven't made our mark,
> the more we try to make it:
> with extravagant language,
> dress,
> haircuts,
> and cosmetics,
> extravagant houses,

and 'big deals':
all trying to prove
we've made it.

Vandalism – wrong as it is –
is often people trying to make their mark,
who feel unable to make it
any other way.

A 'don't care' society –
that doesn't care whether people make their mark –
will be made to care.

And people who say:
'I've made my mark:
You could have made yours, if you'd tried'
will be made to care
profoundly.

Some people never feel they've sexually
made their mark;
and make a smash-and-grab raid
on that kind of achievement:
either in fantasy, or actuality, or both.

Some people from their first days
have felt they never could make their mark,
since mother never showed they'd made their mark with
    her,
and she'd never made her mark of care on them.

Some people need a gang
to help them make their mark,
and never could make it alone.
(Sometimes a gang's more nicely called a 'club'
– with tie and reunion dinner.
Sometimes a gang's a 'Party'.)

Some people make it in a teenage gang,
and then, for the first time,
meet someone for whom they're 'everything':

with whom they've made their mark;
and, at a stroke, the gang life,
and all the teenage delinquency,
disappears.

Politicians
are often like little children,
striving to make their mark;
and so are rich tycoons.
'Even if *I* can't,
my yacht will make my mark,
or my Mercedes.'

And some there be
who're so afraid to make their mark,
they stay concealed
within the pin-stripes of conformity.

Perfect love casts out fear
of never making our mark.

But no love, Lord, except yours,
is ever perfect;
and your love is never perfectly received,
or understood.

So here I am –
and here are all of us –
always fearful,
to some degree,
of not making our mark:
at a party,
in our job,
with the opposite sex,
(and the same one),
and . . .
with You.

So, something of the vandal remains,
always,
in me:

the man who makes his mark
by different kinds of violence.

Kings do it;
policemen do it;
broadcasters and journalists do it;
prison governors, warders and prisoners do it;
judges do it;
clowns and clergy do it.

We were all made to make our mark –
and, somehow, miss it:
or make too large a mark –
for fear of being too small.

Lord, there's something of the vandal in us all.

———— • ◆ • ————

19

Peace and beauty – and messy realities

Wednesday 30 August 1995

During the night I happened to be listening – as I often do – to the
World Service of the BBC. Just before 3 a.m., there was a beautiful
programme on a Grieg violin sonata. It was a very lyrical piece of
music, reflecting all that we mean by the 'Song of Norway'. But it
spoke of more than that. Indeed, it sang of peace and beauty.

At three, on the hour, there was a news bulletin, with news of the
expected air attack by planes of NATO and the United Nations on
military targets. The news was followed by a spokesman defending
the attack. He used two words which stood out in stark contrast to

that Grieg violin sonata. He talked of 'messy realities'. He described in detail the difficult decisions which had been taken. There were some details, he said, he couldn't go into, for the planes involved hadn't yet returned to their bases.

I switched off my bedside wireless, and lay quiet and still in the darkness.

'Peace and beauty' . . . 'messy realities', I thought. And I thought of people involved on the ground and in the skies. And it seemed for a moment that all my life those two worlds had been alongside each other: 'Peace and beauty'; 'messy realities'.

When I was twelve, I joined something called 'The Peace Pledge Union'. We wore a badge which simply said 'War: We Say No'. But war came – in two years. During the war, I would sometimes cross the Thames at lunchtime, from the riverside wharf where I worked, and listen to, for instance, Archbishop William Temple. He said it was a Christian thing to take up arms on behalf of oppressed people. He asked us to consider the Christian's duty when the lives of several million Jews were at risk. And in 1945 – 50 years ago – came Hiroshima and Nagasaki.

One day, when I was training for ordination, the Dean of my College said to me: 'Eric, you're a romantic, and you won't survive unless you have a very high doctrine of corruption in Church and State.' Well, over the years, I've developed that 'high doctrine of corruption'. It's manifest on all sides: in politicians and priests and military people; in people in power as well as in the little people.

But corruption is not the whole story. There's also that 'Song of Norway', of 'Peace and beauty'. And on a morning like this, the least one can do is to pray that that song may yet be heard within and above the 'messy realities'; and that our human corruption may be forgiven and done away with.

———— •◆• ————

20

The Peace Process

Thursday 7 September 1995

This morning we might have been mulling over the first fruits of the Downing Street talks on the Peace Process. And no one should underestimate the seriousness of their cancellation. But at such a time it's worth reminding ourselves that concern for peace in Ireland is to be found, not least, wherever Irish immigrants are gathered together. Last week, in Warrington, a special organization – Warrington–Ireland Reconciliation Enterprise – was initiated. Warrington had, of course, suffered grievously in what we euphemistically call 'an incident'.

Today, I travel to Glasgow, well aware that the rivalry between, for instance, Rangers and Celtic, often emanates from Irish immigrants, who continue their Irish feud in a rather more friendly form on foreign soil. I'm travelling to that great city to meet the new leader of the Iona Community. 'Iona?' you may say: 'That's surely pure Scotland.'

No. St Columba himself set out from Ireland for the island of Iona in 563, with twelve companions, and remained there for virtually the rest of his life.

In 1938, Dr George MacLeod left his slum parish in Govan, in Glasgow, to seek new and radical ways of living the Gospel in today's world. The rebuilding of the ancient Abbey of Iona – with the aid of unemployed craftsmen – was one of his first ambitions. The Community he founded is now a network of 200 members, 1000 associates, and 2000 friends. They come from all walks of life: ordained and lay; Protestant and Catholic; men and women; and are scattered about the world They are bound together by a common rule of spiritual and economic discipline, commitment to prayer, and to work for justice and peace. They have the Peace Process among the Irish, wherever they are, close to their heart.

It was when I was a student that Iona first drew me. I spent several weeks there, just before I was ordained; and the inspiration of that time has been with me for over 40 years. And I speak today about the Iona Community because the Peace Process can so easily *sound* like something carried on only by top politicians – indeed, it can *be* like that. But I believe it's something in which we can all play a part, and in which the Iona Community has set us an example – sustained as it is by attention to the Life of the Spirit, which that ancient Abbey of Iona still signifies and represents.

Iona's Abbey is what the poet Philip Larkin would have called 'a serious house on serious earth', which in recent years has surprised in many 'a hunger to be more serious', not least about peace and justice and the Peace Process.

———◆———

21

St Martin-in-the-Fields

Thursday 14 September 1995

Last night I went to the Induction of the new vicar of what is, I suppose, Britain's most famous parish church: St Martin-in-the-Fields. Of course, it hasn't been 'in the fields' for centuries; it's in Trafalgar Square. Central London will be a very different field of work for the new vicar, Nick Holtam, who, for the past several years, has been working in the Isle of Dogs, an area of dramatic re-development and immense social problems, in London's East End.

The new vicar of St Martin's enters a great tradition, of course. When its most famous vicar, Dick Sheppard, was appointed in 1914, the church was of little importance in the religious life of London. Dick soon made it a name throughout Britain, and, indeed, the Commonwealth; and it's held that position ever since.

Dick Sheppard was a very remarkable character. He loved the Church, but was very critical of it. He called his most famous book *The Impatience of a Parson*. He was deeply religious, but he was also brimful of fun and mischief. He acted for a while as secretary to the then Archbishop of York. That was 80 years ago, when class distinctions were more obvious and stiff. One day, Dick told the Archbishop he wanted to play golf with the butler. The Archbishop said that would never do. That day there was a procession in the Minster in which Dick had to carry the processional cross in front of the Archbishop, as he led him to his throne. As they started off in the procession, Dick whispered to the Archbishop: 'May I play golf with the butler?' The request was ignored. Dick repeated the request, but added: 'If you don't say "Yes", I shall lead you down into the crypt.' The Archbishop, knowing that Dick was quite capable of carrying out his threat, reluctantly caved in.

It was from St Martin-in-the-Fields that Dick conducted the first religious service ever broadcast. It was relayed on the first Sunday evening of 1924. Dick Sheppard probably gave as great an impetus to religious broadcasting as any other parson has ever done, and every vicar of St Martin's since Dick Sheppard has continued that ministry.

But broadcasting wasn't Dick's only gift. He made it clear that St Martin's was open to all who needed comfort, courage and sympathy when in trouble. There was a welcome for all manner of people, especially the lonely and the lost. Dick had teased the Archbishop about the crypt at York; but it was the crypt of St Martin's that he made famous throughout the world, for the food and shelter it provided for all in need. That work has not only gone on, it has grown over the years. St Martin's is still a magnificent church. It's an example of living worship. But it's the silent partnership of worship and social care which I think speaks volumes.

———— • ◆ • ————

22

Sleep, Holy Babe

Friday 8 December 1995

You may have seen that the BBC, this year, is providing for BBC 1 viewers, on Christmas Eve, an updated version of the Nativity, in strip cartoon style. From time to time, poets, playwrights and parsons have portrayed Jesus as 'our contemporary'. But what about Mary and Joseph?

Well, if Mary remained single today, during her pregnancy, she could claim a single person's income support – though she would have to remain available for work, and be actively seeking it, to get the benefit; and, if she was under eighteen, she could only claim support on a discretionary basis of hardship. Once she'd had her baby, she'd be able to claim at the rate for those over 25 – along with the Lone Parent Premium. And once she and Joseph were married, and living together, they could claim £75.20 a week for themselves – assuming both of them were unemployed and had no savings – plus £10.55 Family Premium.

And when Jesus was born, Mary could claim a one-off maternity payment – to cover bedding, pram, furniture, and so on. She could also claim Child Benefit – that's if Jesus was the eldest child – and she could claim that, whether she was on benefit or not.

The income of Joseph and Mary from Income Support would be £86 a week; but this would have to cover all expenses – from food, heating and electricity, to clothes, shoes and travel.

If Joseph's carpentry was casual, not full-time, and Mary did a bit of sewing and cleaning on the side, they'd be able to keep £15 a week of the extra money. After that they'd begin to lose benefit. When they declared their earnings, they might find their benefit suspended until adjustment had been made, leaving them perhaps with no benefit at all for a fortnight or so.

To cover housing costs they could probably claim housing benefit – assuming they'd managed to find 'a place of their own'. Mary wouldn't have an automatic right to a home as a single parent. And, of course, many private landlords refuse people on benefit house-room – especially if there are children. Mary and Joseph could easily end up in bed and breakfast – that's if their local authority accepted them as homeless.

There are, of course, advantages to sleeping in a stable – not least the natural animal heating. And there's no VAT on that.

If they happened to be victims of some modern Herod, it would be little use their coming to Britain after 8 January. They'd probably be called 'bogus asylum seekers'. Certainly Joseph's dream wouldn't get him very far as 'reasonable fear of persecution'.

Christmas challenges each one of us to think how Jesus 'our contemporary' – and Mary and Joseph – should be cared for today, through the state and the churches and the various charitable bodies. But many people, it has to be said, prefer to keep Jesus cribbed and cradled in the first century – or at the latest the fifteenth – in a Botticelli sort of stable. 'For God's sake don't let him affect life today,' they say, 'Keep him away from our realities.' Sleep, Holy Babe!

23

Children and crime

Friday 15 December 1995

It's a week today since the tragic murder of the head teacher, Philip Lawrence. I've rarely known an event which has caused more people to feel so helpless, and often to say, rather helplessly, 'What can we do?' That helplessness has, of course, been greatly increased by events in Brixton on Wednesday evening.

It would surely be appropriate if, in response to the killing of Philip Lawrence, a number of us undertook some further piece of education that might enable us to do something – however small – to turn back the tide of delinquency.

It so happens that a book has just been published which I believe could be the very resource for this further education that we need. It's called simply *Children and Crime*, and it's by Bob Holman, who's had a rather remarkable life. Growing up during the Second World War, he was evacuated from his East End home eight times, and his family were bombed out twice. The experience had a profound effect on him and led him to train as a child welfare officer. He later went into academic life and, eventually, became a Professor of Social Administration. But increasingly concerned about the remoteness of academics from the problems they study, he moved to Europe's largest public housing estate, Easterhouse in Glasgow, to live alongside the disadvantaged in society. He's now been there for over eight years.

This book is not written for experts. It's aimed at those of us who may lack formal qualifications, but who want to do anything we can to help. He writes: 'I'm convinced that in the long run, the main means of preventing juvenile crime rests with caring people in strong communities.' Bob Holman's a Christian, but his faith is not 'exclusive'. 'Jesus,' he writes, 'was not a distant teacher. His example was that of the involved mixer.'

His book is a mine of provocative information, without being full of statistics. In 1992 he was writing: 'This week, 400,000 sixteen-year-olds leave school: a quarter are likely to join the 100,000 who left school last year and have never worked. How will they pass their evenings?' Bob Holman makes you think alongside them. And, of course, a considerable percentage of them are black young people, in places like Brixton.

It's not often that I believe a Thought for the Day should be largely a recommendation to read a book. But on this occasion I suggest it, first as an act of thanksgiving for Philip Lawrence; then, to increase our mutual understanding and trust in the community; but also as a practical act of intercession for the many young unemployed people of our land – not least, those who are black.

24

Where all the love comes from

Friday 22 December 1995

Several people have said to me, in the last few days: 'The sooner Christmas is over, the better.' That's very sad; but in each case there was some reason for their saying it. Christmas only heightens some people's alone-ness. All the meeting up of families and friends under-lines the fact that they are on their own; and, if they go to someone else, they feel – wrongly, probably – that may be rather forced. For others, sickness in the family dominates their scene. I know of families with children seriously ill and others with an aged parent in hospital.

At midday today, I help at the funeral of a much-loved physician. I can't just say 'Happy Christmas' to his widow. Last night I was priv-ileged to preach at a service in the Chapel at Heathrow for the relatives of those who were killed in the Lockerbie disaster, seven years ago – at Christmas time. Each Christmas now reminds them of their loss. And I know another person who simply cannot afford any presents this year for his children. Others' spending at Christmas reminds him of his poverty.

But all these sad situations, I think, force us to face again just what Christmas is about. It's not really about another baby being born 2000 years ago. It's primarily about how the God of Love copes with the suffering, evil and death in his world. That Love is very relevant to each of the sad, even tragic situations I've described. Our Christmas cards, carols and Nativity plays will all have failed if they haven't got that across.

A little while ago, the six-year-old daughter of a friend of mine, who's a doctor, said to him: 'Daddy, can you explain to me how the heart works?' He was overjoyed at her question, and took it very seriously. He sat her down beside him and drew what he thought was a tolerably good drawing of the arteries of the human body, and quite a good diagram of the heart itself. But, when he turned to his daughter, she was looking very puzzled indeed. 'What is it you don't understand, darling?' he asked. 'Daddy,' she said, 'you haven't explained where all the *love* comes from.'

I think Christmas and the cross is God's way of explaining to us all where the Love comes from: that in spite of all appearances – and realities – the Divine Love is at the heart of the world.

———— • ◆ • ————

25

The Cheapside brat

Friday 29 December 1995

Almost everyone knows something about Thomas à Becket, who was killed in Canterbury Cathedral 825 years ago today. We all know about him, not least, because the Canterbury Pilgrims made his shrine one of the most famous in Christendom: and many hospitals – like St Thomas's in London – and many churches were named in his honour.

Then, in our own time, T. S. Eliot has written his great play, *Murder in the Cathedral*, about the martyrdom of Becket. Such a play is a work primarily of the imagination, rather than of history. Eliot imagines the sermon, in Canterbury Cathedral, Thomas preaches on Christmas morning, four days before he's killed. He puts into the mouth of Thomas the words: 'A Christian martyrdom is never an accident.' 'Saints', he says, 'are never made by accident.' And he goes on: 'The true martyr is one who has become the instrument of God . . .'

Yes, I'm sure that's true. But I'd want to say that all of us need to recognize the reality of accident in our lives: of the random element in life, and the fact of coincidence. Faith does not mean ignoring the accidental: the chance meetings, for instance, which make all the difference to our lives, but which are, frankly, part of life's lottery. God isn't a puppet-master playing some sophisticated game with us all. It becomes more and more clear that much of our make-up, for good or ill, is random.

Faith is not least about what we do with the unpredictable raw material of life: where and when we happen to be born; our genetic inheritance; who mothered us and fathered us when we were born – and who was absent in our earliest years.

'Saints are not made by accident.' Nor are they made by ignoring the accidental.

As we approach the end of the Old Year and the beginning of the New, quite a lot of people are full of foreboding as to what the future may hold. Some are fatalistic about it, echoing the remarks which people used to make during the war: 'If a bomb's got your name on it, it'll get you!'

Eliot, in Thomas's sermon, was saying that accident is one ingredient in life, but only one; the other is faith: when, starting from the realities and raw material of life, we seek to discover and co-operate with the will of God. Faith doesn't ignore the roughness and chaos of human history – personal, social, national, international. It begins there; and, by consciously co-operating with God, transforms people and situations.

It transformed Thomas, the 'Cheapside brat' – as one of Eliot's characters called him – into Saint Thomas of Canterbury.

26

Is it war?

Thursday 7 March 1996

Childhood memories can be extraordinarily powerful. I have a memory of exactly 60 years ago today: 7 March 1936. It was a Saturday, I have reason to remember; and on Saturday afternoons, my father would often sit twiddling with the knob of our radio set, to see what was on. Usually, he would end up with a football match; but on this particular afternoon he got a 'foreign' station, on the Continent, which had the chilling sound of Nazi troops marching into the Rhineland, to re-occupy it: the sound of thousands of boots, marching almost as one, on cobbles, and male voices singing in unison.

I remember my father telling my mother what it was. She only uttered four words – with huge anxiety in her voice: 'John, is it war?' My father pooh-poohed the idea, but my mother's fears communicated themselves to me; and I felt sick with anxiety. In March 1936, I was ten years old. My mother's fears harked back to the First World War, in which her brothers had gone off to France. Her fears were justified. You could say that the re-occupation of the Rhineland began the Second World War.

This morning, as I think back over those 60 years, I find myself reflecting on the mystery of being human. In many ways, that day, my mother and father and I were like frightened animals. But that wasn't the whole story. We, like those German soldiers, would, in time, get caught up with the war machines of our respective nations. We also had it in us to work – and go on working – for peace and for a united Europe.

Those of us who are still alive can look back down the arches of the years – 60 of them – and see the issues of war and peace being slowly worked out; but at an appalling price. My parents are long since dead – as are most of those German soldiers.

It's easy, sometimes, to be cynical about what we call 'history'. But my Thought for the Day, with Israel, and Ireland, and Bosnia particularly in mind, is a kind of prayer:

Lord of history and Prince of Peace,
the Peace Process is always yours before it's ours.
Make us aware of the price of peace.
Renew in us your Hope, your Patience,
    and your Impatience.

——— • ◆ • ———

27

The natural is never enough

Tuesday 12 March 1996

Poetry Please on Radio 4 this last Sunday, reminded us that this year
is the centenary of the publication of *A Shropshire Lad*, a small
volume of verse by, of course, A. E. Housman, who was Professor
of Latin at University College, London, when the book was published. It has remained a best-seller all these years; and I suspect that,
this spring, many of us will take down the volume from our shelves
and read again, in thankfulness for Housman, lines like:

> Loveliest of trees, the cherry now
> Is hung with bloom along the bough.

Housman was, in fact, a very sad man. The hymn he wrote for his
own funeral is gloomy beyond words. It prays that we may be
'restored to peace and darkness'.

I often used to think of Housman when I was Chaplain of Trinity
College, Cambridge, in the late 1950s, where he was Professor of
Latin in his later years; and I had rooms near to where he had had
his. The College had planted an avenue of cherry trees in his
memory, which, each year, to use his words, wore 'white for
Eastertide'. But one year, those trees taught me a lesson for life. They
were just about to burst into full bloom when, one afternoon, I
walked among them in the spring sunshine. Next morning the sky
seemed cloudless when I awoke, and I rose up early to visit again that

lovely avenue. Alas, in the night there had been a severe frost, which had turned all the blossom black. Hardly a bough or a branch of bloom had escaped. I could scarcely believe my eyes – or restrain my tears.

The lesson I learnt that day was that the natural is never enough. Death and mortality may be hidden, out of sight, but are always there. Time is a perpetual perishing. As Harry Williams, one-time Dean of Trinity College, Cambridge, wrote: 'All the fragmentary experiences of love and joy and beauty, as we know them on earth, have ever their hands upon their lips bidding adieu.'

Housman's sad world was an honest world. He knew that the natural needs something more for its completion. The finite needs faith to see beyond it. There are tears at the heart of things, and nature itself cannot dry our eyes.

Yet there is much to be thankful for in the present. The crocuses are ablaze in St James's Park – and in my little Kennington garden – this very day now.

———— • ◆ • ————

28

The experience of unemployment

Tuesday 19 March 1996

The organization Church Action on Poverty has been holding a series of 'poverty hearings' around the country, as part of their project *Local People: National Voice*. Today, there'll be a national Poverty Hearing in Westminster, which the Archbishop of Canterbury and Cardinal Hume will attend. The aim is to provide a forum for people to speak for themselves of their experience of poverty.

Just before Christmas, I was asked to attend one of the local hearings, in Gateshead, and to spend a day with people from the surrounding area, almost all of whom were unemployed. Those who were not unemployed were people like myself, who had been invited to hear what those who were had to say. The Roman Catholic Bishop of Hexham and the Anglican Bishop of Newcastle were among those who were there to listen. We gathered in the hall of St Joseph's Roman Catholic Church, Gateshead. Those who were going to share their experiences with us had done a good deal of preparation for the day. All round the hall were pasted-up phrases – like banners – which summed up the experience of unemployment for those with whom we were meeting. I made a note of some of them:

Lack of self-respect
Feeling like a second-class citizen
Lack of control over one's life
Isolation
Strained relationships in the home
Loss of hope
The struggle to manage, week after week
The inability to replace ordinary household necessities
Not being able to support the family

The importance of today's national event is, not least, to remind us that the experience of poverty and unemployment does not belong only to people in the more obviously deprived areas. Recently, for instance, I was at a similar meeting to the Gateshead gathering at Hastings.

Often, unemployed and poverty-stricken people are, understandably, without hope. But neither the Gateshead nor the Hastings meetings lacked hope. Honesty and realism seemed to have delivered those who were there from what I will call 'emotional pessimism'. Indeed, the sense of being 'all in it together' seemed to have renewed people's hope and reinvigorated their will to confront their situations, which, humanly speaking, were often hopeless.

What St Paul said – 'Bear ye one another's burdens, and so fulfil the law of Christ' – seemed to have a power in those situations parallel to what it had had in these last days in the tragedy at Dunblane; but St Paul's words had been received not as, so to speak, 'good advice' but as 'iron rations': what you need to hear if you're to survive in this world.

———•◆•———

29

The children

Thursday 23 May 1996

In the last few weeks, I've had a rather distasteful job to do: I've been preparing to close down the 50-year-old charity, Christian Action, with which I myself have been closely associated for half its life. It has meant going through documents, letters, photographs: destroying some, preparing others for safe keeping. There have been some laughs, and a lot of reasons to be thankful; but sometimes, I have to admit, I've been quite near to tears. The death of an institution is, in some ways, like the death of a human being. And 'there's a time to be born, and a time to die'.

It's helped that I've been doing this necessary work in the 40 days after Easter, and I've not been able to take my mind off the question: 'When the organization Christian Action has been laid to rest – and, after all, it's only one charity among many – what form should Christian social action take in Britain today, and in the world at large?'. In fact, I've been producing an edition of our journal to ask just that question, and to try to provide some answers. I wrote to several people I know in responsible positions in society, and asked them to try and answer the question. One MP has worked hard at it; so too has the Leader of the Iona Community, that wonderful group of people who work both on the Scottish mainland and on that romantic and historic island; a community worker from Wales has provided her experience and insights; so too has Bruce Kent who has been working unflaggingly on the disarmament question for decade upon decade.

But I'm particularly glad that one morning I had a kind of brainwave. I got a friend of mine who's a gifted photographer to go into the primary school near our office and photograph the children at work and at play in Kennington – that's to say, inner-city Lambeth – where the children nowadays come from many different social backgrounds.

Those photographs are, in fact, their own answers to my question: 'What should be the future of Christian social action?' It's a two-word answer: 'The children.' It's not of course a final or detailed answer; it's only the beginning of one. But I doubt whether there's a more important answer that any party political broadcast could give, or any church leader, or any spokesperson for a charity. Education, housing, poverty, employment, health, race, family welfare – they're all there, in 'the children'.

No wonder Jesus himself took a child and stood that child in front of everyone, and said, 'There's your future.'

30

The Old Bailey

Thursday 30 May 1996

Recently, one of the judges in my congregation at Gray's Inn, where I'm what's called the 'Preacher', asked me whether I'd like to be shown around the Old Bailey some time, where she sits in court most days of the year. I immediately said I would, and, last evening, through her good offices, I was invited to join a group of people going round, and spent a fascinating few hours there.

What we were shown was, in effect, a history of the pursuit of justice in this country. There's been, of course, a huge change since the treatment of prisoners on the Old Bailey site was brutal beyond words. A statue of Elizabeth Fry there powerfully makes the point, reminding you of the pioneers of prison reform, not least among women prisoners and children. It's now a very busy series of courts, with nearly 2000 cases a year, and about 3000 people a day going in and out of the building.

In such surroundings, you can't help having in mind some of the great trials there: Oscar Wilde, Crippen, the Kray brothers, and so on. And I was reminded of some of the great advocates my father used always to be talking about – like Sir Patrick Hastings. And, of course, nowadays you half expect to see Rumpole of the Bailey appearing through some archway.

If part of the life of the Bailey seems steeped in history, other parts of it clearly could not be more up to date, with all the resources of modern technology – tape recorders and video cameras – to assist the processes of justice.

And when you've seen everything there's to be seen inside, there remains, of course, the huge Figure of Justice crowning the court and towering above the City: an instantly recognizable symbol, now, because of films and the TV news. The Figure of Justice is not blind-folded, as some maintain.

Over the main entrance is a text from the Book of Psalms – common, of course, to Jews and Christians. 'Defend the children of the poor,' it says, 'and punish the wrongdoer.' That text rather mar-vellously underlines how our British pursuit of social and criminal justice relates to our religious roots. But it also hints at the human tragedies which are played out every day at the Bailey, and at the other courts of our land.

Yet my evening also taught me something about myself – or, rather, about everyone of us. One of the most marvellous aspects of our humanity is surely our human ability to go on striving and strug-gling for justice. It's an ability, like our other abilities, that we can either exercise or neglect. But it's not something we can simply leave to others – like judges or politicians. The Psalmist is telling us that, where justice is concerned, we all have our part to play.

31

Do this

Thursday 6 June 1996

Not long ago, I met someone who said to me, 'You're Eric James, aren't you?' I pleaded guilty, and he said, 'I always think of you as the *Sixties* Eric James.' I smiled, and he went on: 'You see, I remember an article you wrote in the Sixties.' In fact, it was one of a series of articles I wrote for an *avant garde* journal called *Prism*.

When I looked at those articles again a few days ago, I found I didn't want to revise them, and they seemed particularly appropriate for today. You see, lots of people keep today as the Feast of Corpus Christi, which simply means 'The Body of Christ'; and those articles I wrote in the Sixties were all on that theme.

I was reminding readers of that journal, that Jesus gave very few commands, but that there was one which was as good an example of a 'direct command' as you could find. He said, 'Do this in remembrance of me'; and the Church has gone on doing it faithfully and unfailingly: taking bread as he did, breaking it, and sharing it.

The person I met in the street said I'd reminded him how simple and direct and unavoidable Jesus' command was. But I'd gone on to say that it's one thing to be certain about Jesus' command, but quite another to be clear what he had in mind when he gave that command.

St Paul wrote that we were to do what Jesus said 'in remembrance of him'; but that word 'remembrance' is very slippery. Sometimes we think of 'remembrance' as the recollection of someone absent from us; but the Greek and Hebrew equivalents of our Bible word mean much more than that: the events recalled become alive and powerful for us. So, 'Do this in remembrance of me' is an instruction to remember what a great Roman Catholic theologian called 'The Whole Christ'. But too often the Christ we remember is too small.

This is what I wrote in the Sixties: 'Jesus says, "This is my Body". He is saying it over all his creation . . .' This can, of course, be the most romantic nonsense – sheer pietism, flying in the face of the facts.

Here is a seven-year-old child, dying of leukaemia. 'My body?' Yes and No.

When Christ says, 'This is my body', he is saying 'Yes' – because I made this, and 'Yes' because I've done all that could ever be done for it to be transformed into what I have always intended it to be; and 'Yes' because if you seek me you will find me in this body. And 'No' because this body is not yet as Christ intended it to be.

But there's never a moment, never a situation, in which we're not able to say, 'This is my body'. Every day and every place is Corpus Christi.

———— ◆ ————

32

I'm not talking to you

Thursday 13 June 1996

One of the oldest and most famous clubs in London is called 'The Beefsteak'. It has its premises just off Leicester Square. It's a pity that, with such a name, *this particular year* it's celebrating the centenary of its occupying that site. But, who knows, perhaps 'The Beefsteak' has something to contribute to the removal of the European ban on our beef; and, indeed, something to teach us all. For one of the rules of 'The Beefsteak' is that you sit together at one long table, taking your place in the order in which you arrive: sitting next to whoever happens to be already seated; and you talk with them. It's a club that rates very highly not just eating, but meeting and conversation. A ban on talking to one another at 'The Beefsteak' would be as serious as a ban on beef itself, and of course, there are many who maintain that what's needed now, in the 'beef war', is more talk: not least, say some, about the disposal of carcasses.

When I was a child, I can so well remember on one occasion being roundly rebuked by my mother when I simply said to my younger sister: 'I'm not talking to you.'

Later, it was one of my mentors who taught me that conversation is like playing dominoes. 'When someone puts down a five in conversation,' he said, 'see whether you've got a five. If they put down a six, you should try and find a six. Wherever you eat, whoever you're put next to, find what you have in common. Divisions and differences will be plain enough.'

It's therefore not altogether surprising that at one time the word 'conversation' meant much more than exchanging words. It meant how you behaved: indeed, how you acted as a citizen. It even meant sexual intimacy.

So St Paul, writing to the Philippians, says: 'Let your conversation be worthy of the Gospel of Christ', meaning, of course, more than words; meaning conduct. He even says, 'Our conversation is in heaven', again meaning 'our whole way of life'.

Yes; perhaps 'The Beefsteak' has something to say to us at this centenary. Whoever we're next to; whatever their race or sex or class, our conversation with them – our behaviour – is of huge importance. And it's sad, I think, that the meal table is fast disappearing from so many homes. It's when we sit next to people, talk with them, eat with them, stay with them, that we discover who they are – and who we are. And dialogue at the highest political level in, say, Ireland, Jerusalem, Brussels or Bosnia, has a lot to learn from conversation at table.

———— •◆• ————

33

Risk

Wednesday 4 September 1996

Recently I was asked whether I'd give a talk on the subject of 'Risk'. That night, I woke up suddenly, and I couldn't get back to sleep, and decided to use the notebook I always keep at my bedside, to make some notes on 'Risk'. I was astonished how quickly the pages filled. Almost all the virtues could be related to risk: courage, wisdom, patience – and all the vices: fear, foolishness, indiscretion.

Risk seemed to be related to the unknown; to our identity, sexuality, relationship; to exploration, to banking and business; painting and preaching; moving house and changing jobs; and to crime. I was amazed how much of life was related to risk – even going to sleep: 'perchance to dream'.

I got to sleep again; but when I came downstairs in the morning to collect the paper, I found that Saddam Hussein had been up to no good. He'd been invading areas of Iraq controlled by the Kurds, and it was clear he'd risked military and economic reprisals by the USA. Already the Americans were working out reprisals which would have their own quota of risk – and we know now that guided missiles were their response, twice.

Of course, it isn't only the members of the military machines, so to speak – on both sides – who have, calculatedly or rashly, risked. The lives of the innocent, as always, were also at risk. Missiles are rarely as accurate as they claim to be. And there are political as well as military risks in the USA as well as in Iraq.

I always have a pile of books to read which I haven't been able to get through. Yesterday, I began one by Grace Sheppard, wife of the Bishop of Liverpool. Suddenly one sentence seemed to jump out at me from the text: 'He risked misunderstanding of his role as an all-powerful God by wearing a crown of thorns, and also by putting a towel round his waist, and washing the feet of his disciples . . .' I found myself wondering whether in this fraught international situation risk only belongs to the seemingly all-powerful. I suspect we ought also to be thinking of those who inescapably are wearing a crown of thorns – and those who have taken a towel and girded themselves: those 30 British humanitarian aid workers, for instance, who have been trying to take some costly initiatives of service. Let's pray, not least, that their work will neither be ignored nor undone.

·———◆———·

34

Members one of another

Wednesday 11 September 1996

This last weekend, I preached in the Chapel of Haddo House, near Aberdeen. The house stands amid acres of estate.

Yesterday, I visited the family of an unemployed miner, at Seaham, County Durham, on the coast, near Sunderland, where the mines used to extend three miles under the sea.

You might think there was no connection between those two events. And if I tell you that, at Haddo House, I slept in the bedroom where Archie Gordon, the youngest son of the seventh Earl of Aberdeen was born, who'd been buried from the Chapel where I was preaching, after he'd died, at 25, from the injuries he'd suffered in a car crash outside Winchester, in 1909, you might be forgiven for still thinking there was no obvious connection between the two events.

Archie Gordon and Violet Asquith, the then Prime Minister's daughter, got engaged in the hospital ward at Winchester, hours before he died. She was, of course, very bereaved, and attended his funeral in the Chapel at Haddo. In Archie's memory, Violet founded a boys' club in Hoxton, in the slums of East London, and there's no doubt that running that club – from 10 Downing Street, of all places – helped her overcome the loss of Archie.

In Violet's recently published diary, edited by Mark Bonham Carter, there occurs this entry for 10 November 1910:

> 10 Downing Street. Just back from the Club, where my life seems to centre more and more. Slightly jarred by Winnie and Clemmie [Churchill, of course] who came downstairs and sat with me while I had my supper – talking about my 'good works'. 'Good works' – my God, how little they know! How dare they touch on my sacredest joy and call it 'good works'.
>
> It's a little odd to me . . . to feel so little curiosity or interest or responsibility about other people's lives as most people I know do. I can never remember not feeling it – not being haunted by the thought of the poor and longing to do something . . . I'm about as self-centred and as self-indulgent as it's possible for a human being to be – yet I'm haunted and obsessed by the thought of the squalor and greyness and sunlessness of some lives – and by the arbitrariness with which our fates are dealt round.

Violet Asquith would, I'm sure, have seen the clear connection between my preaching in Haddo Chapel on Sunday and visiting that poverty-stricken family in Seaham yesterday. She would have hoped to find her longing to do something for the poor, and her sense of responsibility for other people's lives, in us all – whatever our political or, indeed, ecclesiastical allegiance.

She knew well what St Paul meant by being 'members one of another'.

35

The truth of humanity

Wednesday 18 September 1996

The only church committee I now belong to – in my seventies – is one that looks after clergy who've been in trouble. And I nearly didn't belong to that, because one of its members came up to me and said: 'I hear you're joining us on the Delinquent Clergy Committee.' I said, 'I'd only be willing to join such a committee if it was clear that it looked after *fellow* delinquent clergy.'

I wasn't being tetchy. To me it's a fundamental point that every priest is, to some extent, a failed priest. And since one of the main tasks of a priest is to hold up to people the meaning of being human, I suspect that when a priest, or a bishop, or an archbishop, or a cardinal fails, the hearts of lots of people, and their prayers, will go out to them, because they'll recognize in that failure something which they know only too well in themselves.

A great French priest, Père Teilhard de Chardin – who was in fact ordained in England, in Hastings, Sussex-by-the-Sea – wrote in a book on priesthood:

> To the full extent of my power, because I am a priest, I wish from now on to be the first to become conscious of all that the world loves, pursues and suffers. I want to be the first to seek, to sympathise and to suffer: the first to open myself out and sacrifice myself – to become more widely human and more nobly of the earth than any of the world's servants.

There speaks a priest of this century, who, I believe, is speaking the truth of priesthood which this century waits to hear. For in the truth of priesthood there is the truth of humanity itself: the truth about us all. To me it's a particularly powerful passage, not least because it holds together 'all that the world loves' and also speaks of the significance of sacrifice.

Next Monday, I shall make my way to Liverpool – to Liverpool's Anglican Cathedral – to join all those who will be giving thanks for the life and ministry of the young priest, Christopher Gray, who was murdered late one night recently at his vicarage, in the course of his duties. I don't myself doubt that Christopher Gray was profoundly fulfilled in his life and ministry as a priest. I do not doubt also that he would have wanted to speak of himself – as I have to speak of myself – as a delinquent priest, who needed to go to confession from time to time and receive absolution.

To be a priest is to be human: to be human is to be a priest.

———— •◆• ————

36

A lonely life

Wednesday 25 September 1996

The activities of bishops seem to have captured quite a lot of the headlines lately; and this week the biography of the most colourful bishop of our time will be published: Mervyn Stockwood, Bishop of Southwark for 21 years, from 1959 to 1980.

He recruited to the episcopate and to his staff people like John Robinson, author of the Sixties best-seller *Honest to God*, and David Sheppard, erstwhile captain of England's cricket team, now Bishop of Liverpool. Mervyn Stockwood made a huge impact on the inner-city Diocese of Southwark. But it's the sub-title of the perceptive biography by Michael De-la-Noy that intrigues me. He calls it *A Lonely Life*. Mervyn Stockwood is, of course, not the only bishop to be described that way. He was lonely not least because you never quite knew where you were with him – and I speak as one who was thought to have been close to him for twenty years and more.

He was a contradictory character. He said he was a socialist, but was happy hob-nobbing with the royals and the lords. He was, nevertheless, one of the greatest parish priests of this century, in one of the poorest parishes in Bristol.

He could, in turn, enthral and exasperate; be kind and arrogant; compassionate and cruel. He could consume more alcohol than almost anyone I've known; yet when he decided to give it up, he could – and did.

Friendship was of huge importance to him; but you never quite knew when he'd stab you in the back. He was in chapel early each day, and lived a deeply devout and disciplined life, and inspired much affection and respect.

He was homosexual and he wasn't good with women – and the exceptions proved the rule. He was aware of his faults but could rarely admit them.

On a trip to the Holy Land, when someone accused him of being 'two people', he simply smiled and said: 'Two? I'm 22!'

I've never known anyone to hold up such a clear mirror to our human complexity. And perhaps it's important that someone, from time to time, should rid us of our illusions and unreality not only about who they are but who all of us human beings are – by our creation.

One of the great French spiritual directors, the Abbé de Tourville, said:

> Remember: perfection never exists apart from imperfection: just as good health cannot exist without our feeling effort, fatigue, heat or cold, hunger or thirst. Yet none of those prevent the enjoyment of good health.

. . . or our answering the invitation to spiritual progress – in which may lie the answer to our loneliness.

37

Growth in Godliness

Saturday 16 November 1996

One of the best books I've ever read is called *The Foolishness of God* – a phrase, you may remember, of St Paul. The author of the book is John Austin Baker, who for some years was Chairman of the Church of England's Doctrine Commission, and for eleven years was Bishop of Salisbury. He retired three years ago, and in retirement has just produced another splendid book, simply called *The Faith of a Christian*, which he has rather movingly dedicated to the 'many friends in whom during my lifetime I have seen so much of the face of Christ, and especially to my dear wife'.

It's a very creative and courageous book John Austin Baker has now written – not least, for instance, in what he writes about the vexed question of homosexuality. 'Christians,' he writes, 'need to reappraise the issue of homosexuality . . . To the detached observer' he continues, 'the most obvious feature of Christian sexual teaching is that it is an ethic for heterosexuals. Given that the overwhelming majority of the human race is heterosexual that's reasonable enough. 'But,' he says, 'it means that this ethic can be fairly applied to homosexuals only by classifying them as deviant heterosexuals; and that, in the light of increasing knowledge, is no longer reasonable.'

'Like many other developments in Nature,' John Austin Baker concludes, 'homosexuality is simply a fact. What matters is to ask how best it can be enabled to further God's purposes, and here again,' he says, 'the key concept is growth in godliness.'

The Bishop has written, in my judgement, just the few pages which were needed to bring calm to a debate which is so often ruled, and indeed ruined, by passion. And I say that purposely today because this very evening in Southwark Cathedral there's to be a service which is meant primarily to give thanks for an organization which, for twenty years now, has endeavoured to enable homosexual people to grow in godliness.

As John Austin Baker writes:

Even a modest acquaintance with those living with HIV or AIDS will discover outstanding instances of Christlikeness. The sacrificial devotion of many who are gay to their sick or dying partners, and the courage of the sufferers themselves, witness that their love has been a means of grace by which they have grown into true godliness. They have redeemed suffering and evil, and refused to be defeated by death.

It's good that, at this time, John Austin Baker should remind us all that our sexuality – heterosexual or homosexual – is to further God's purposes and to enable us to grow in godliness.

38

Brief encounter

Saturday 23 November 1996

If I say 'Brief Encounter', I expect you'll think of that marvellous Noel Coward film, with Celia Johnson and Trevor Howard. I can't see it too often. But the 'Brief Encounter' I have in mind this morning wasn't a film, it was 'real life', as they say. It was, in fact, with someone I only met once, but the other day, when I opened my newspaper, there was the news of his death – at a young age.

It was over twenty years ago when we had our one and only meeting – but I shan't ever forget it – or him. He was in guard's officer's uniform. We had a late-night meal together in what was then the Strand Corner House. He was 20 then; I was already twice his age – and more. He told me that evening a great deal about himself: about the schoolmaster who most influenced him; that he'd been 'sent down' from Oxford; that he was mad keen on show-jumping. It intrigued us both that when that year I was preaching on Good Friday, he would be riding. I remember his saying with a smile that his world was cavalry, mine Calvary. He was as keen on words as I. He loved acting, particularly Shakespeare. We'd got talking not least because he'd put his wallet on top of his car when he had to stop somewhere on Salisbury Plain, and had driven off forgetting it, and only in that Corner House had he suddenly realized he hadn't the wherewithal to pay for a meal.

After our meeting, I remember, I caught the last train back to St Albans, where I was living then.

I count that one meeting one of the most unforgettable encounters of my life. And the news of his death – in his forties – left me as bereaved as I've been of people I've known for years.

I couldn't get to his funeral; but I spent some time thinking of him, and, of course, praying for him; and it suddenly struck me how many of the encounters Jesus had might be described as 'brief encounters': sudden meetings with strangers – like mine with my now dead friend. There was Zacchaeus, the Woman taken in Adultery, the Widow of Nain, the Two Thieves either side of him on the cross, and so on.

In our experiences of human friendship, however brief, we gain glimpses of the love of God. 'Now,' in this world, says St Paul, 'we know in part.' But the cross of Calvary teaches us all we need to know of the friendship of Christ for each one of us.

———— •◆• ————

39

We are the music makers

Saturday 30 November 1996

The choral tradition in Britain is a remarkable phenomenon, and not least the enthusiasm for singing *Messiah*. In cities and towns large and small, throughout the length and breadth of the British Isles, groups of people are preparing to sing Handel's *Messiah* to celebrate Christmas. It dates back to its first performance in 1742, which took place, not in London, but in Dublin, and not in either of Dublin's two cathedrals, or in one of its many churches, but in the Fishamble Street Musick Hall, which had just been opened.

It was William Cavendish, the Duke of Devonshire, an energetic patron of the arts, who asked his friend Handel to provide him with an oratorio. On such things as patronage great music and great musicians then – as now – often depended. The sacred still had to be paid for in secular cash. And as for *Messiah* being delivered in a music hall: perhaps that's not inappropriate for one who was born in a manger. Handel had devised an oratorio in a simple transportable form which did not require huge orchestral forces, but did require what money could not command: the genius of Handel.

He was in his fifty-seventh year. He'd lived his last eighteen years in London, for most of them a naturalized citizen. His English was still broken, but his first thoughts were as often in English as German. In 1737 he'd suffered a stroke, and his right side had been partially paralysed; but he'd made a remarkable recovery, and his playing and composing were little affected. Handel wrote 40 operas, five oratorios, and numerous sacred and secular choral works. No other composer in Europe had half so much music in print.

We all too often take music for granted – even *great* music. We may even say with the poet O'Shaughnessy: 'We are the music makers.' But we need to reflect from time to time, on the very nature of music; on its mystery; on the nature of musical inspiration and appreciation, and what that has to say about the nature of our humanity. When a human being composes such a work as *Messiah*, he says something about the nature of us all. He exalts us all. When we perform or appreciate *Messiah*, we say something about who we are. 'Say it with music' is more than a Thirties signature tune. Music is the signature that reveals some of the heights and depths of our humanity.

———————◆———————

40

Christian Action

Saturday 7 December 1996

This afternoon, in St Paul's Cathedral, there's to be a service of thanksgiving to bring to a conclusion the work of the charity Christian Action, which began with a huge meeting in Oxford Town Hall exactly 50 years ago.

Clement Atlee, when he was Prime Minister, appointed the initiator of that meeting, John Collins, to a Canonry at St Paul's; and he stayed there for 38 years, becoming a national figure and one of the world's leading protagonists in the cause of social justice and peace. Christian Action, under John Collins's leadership, played a great part in, for instance, the campaign to abolish capital punishment. He was always at the forefront of the Aldermaston March at Eastertide, which was part of the Campaign for Nuclear Disarmament.

But perhaps his greatest achievement came after he visited South Africa in 1956 and began to raise money on behalf of the opponents of apartheid who had been arrested and imprisoned. This was to pay for their legal defence and to provide support for their families. The outrage of the shootings at Sharpeville in 1960 made the task of fund-raising in Britain a good deal easier.

Christian Action had often achieved its aims by founding new charities, and the separate anti-apartheid charity that was set up was known as International Defence and Aid. It soon became one of the chief instruments outside South Africa for the defeat of apartheid. Nelson Mandela, before he was arrested and imprisoned for 27 years, slipped out of South Africa and called on John Collins at St Paul's to ask him to mobilize all the help from Britain that he could.

When Canon Collins retired, not long before his death, I became the Director of Christian Action, and have been privileged to lead it for seventeen years. It was in that position that I was able to appeal to Robert Runcie, the then Archbishop of Canterbury, thirteen years ago to set up his Commission on Urban Priority Areas, which eventually produced the report *Faith in the City*.

Of course, the work of Christian Action can never be said to be finished. Jesus said, 'The poor you have always with you.' And it's been said, 'Christ will be in agony till the end of time' – in the sufferings of his children.

It's only one organization that's closing down. But perhaps it's appropriate, as Christian Action closes, for us all to ask ourselves what organizations and what work in the world we do or support as our Christian Action, our care for others. Jesus said: 'Inasmuch as ye have done it to the least of these my brethren, ye have done it unto me.'

———•◆•———

41

Mere ritual?

Wednesday 5 March 1997

Last week, I had to preach at the funeral of a friend of mine I'd known for 30 years. By profession he was a soldier. He'd been Colonel of the Staffordshire Regiment, as had his father before him. His regiment wanted to accord him the honour they felt to be his due; so some soldiers were despatched to London from Lichfield, their Staffordshire base, to carry his coffin, which was draped with the Union Jack.

The most moving moments of the service for me were when those soldiers got ready to carry the coffin into the church in Chelsea, and when, at the end of the service, they prepared to shoulder the coffin again and carry it out of the church. The soldiers on the left, facing forward, stretched out their right arms towards the soldiers on their right, and the soldiers on the right stretched out their left arms towards the soldiers on their left, and they gripped one another's shoulders so that it was immediately evident that they were bound together; and, tightly gripping one another, they carried my friend's coffin in slow march.

Ritual can be empty and meaningless. We sometimes speak of 'mere' ritual. But on this occasion the ritual was moving beyond words. The actions spoke louder than any words could have done. And I wasn't alone in feeling that. I heard several of the congregation make a similar comment. But what was the ritual saying? It was certainly saying: 'We belong to one another.' That wouldn't be surprising for members of the same regiment. But I think it was saying more than that. Much more.

When death removes someone from our midst, we are at our most vulnerable and need each other – each other's support. Those soldiers were symbolizing a unity and a solidarity that survives and overcomes death. St Paul said simply 'We are members one of another.'

I had the feeling that if we could but trust that symbol – have faith in it – then nothing could withstand it. It spoke of the bond which is greater than that of a regiment, greater even than the bond of a nation or a race. It spoke of that unity which links the living with the dead, that overcomes death and the fear of death. It spoke of that unity which is ours if we would but claim it – through our God-given humanity, and divinity. 'We are members one of another.'

———•◆•———

42

Sing as we go

Wednesday 12 March 1997

I'm just ending my time as what is called 'Preacher' to the lawyers of Gray's Inn. I've been privileged to be their preacher for nineteen years. At my last service, the choir sang some very joyous music: Schubert's *Mass in G*. I was glad that thereby we were able to play some small part in celebrating what is, this year, the 200th anniversary of Schubert's birth.

No composer did more to make people think of life as a journey. When he was writing that *Mass in G*, he was only 18: it was early in his journey. In fact, Schubert's own journey didn't last long: he died when he was only 31. But what treasure he produced on the way! Six hundred songs, nine symphonies – including the sublime *Unfinished* and the great *C Major* – and a huge quantity of wonderful chamber music. In 1815 alone, when he composed that *Mass in G*, he also composed 144 superb songs – eight on one day.

Schubert's last great song-cycle, the *Winterreise* – the 'Winter's Journey' – most of all makes us think of the journey of life. It's the record of a personal pilgrimage across a frozen landscape towards death. Some people think of it simply as a testament of despair. But if it were only that, the great recordings would surely not have the huge sale that they have and the undeniable popularity.

It's true that, at the last, Schubert leaves us with the sound of an organ-grinder in, so to speak, 'the bleak midwinter'. And, no doubt he saw himself as that solitary organ-grinder, who knew no fame or fortune, or lasting love. And yet that organ-grinder's music has echoed across the continents and down two centuries.

It has echoed and re-echoed because increasingly, it could be said, the music of Franz Schubert was not 'romantic' – in the sense of unrealistic. There's little of what we call avoidance or denial in it. He seems to say, at the end: 'This is how it is.' He offers his journey as company and sympathy for others who travel the same way. So, 200 years on, Schubert's music lives – in a way that Schubert himself would never have dared to believe.

I think people like Schubert force us to define ourselves as music-making animals, and help us, whatever the course of our journey, to 'sing as we go'.

———————•◆•———————

43

Mystique and politique

Wednesday 19 March 1997

'Everything begins in mysticism and ends in politics' wrote the French Catholic writer Charles Péguy. He was meaning that what begins with lofty ideals and spiritual vision has to be brought down to earth by, literally, the vote.

'Men have died for freedom', Péguy wrote, 'and men have died for faith. You say that elections are a ridiculous formality, and you have good reason for saying it; but men have suffered, men have died, a whole people have lived so that today the greatest idiot should have the right to place his vote in the ballot box. Everything begins in mystique and ends in politique.'

Besides thinking of that great French Christian, I find myself thinking today of the great German Christian, Dietrich Bonhoeffer, who met his death in a Nazi concentration camp in 1945 for his involvement in the plot to assassinate Hitler. If anyone tells me that Christians should keep out of politics, I always ask them what they would have done about Hitler – and, if they were alive then, what they *did* about him.

There's a story about Bonhoeffer which I think is peculiarly relevant at this time.

On 14 June 1940, Bonhoeffer, who was then principal of a Protestant seminary, took one of his students, Eberhard Bethge, to a café in Memel, East Prussia. While they were sitting in the garden of the café, the news came over the radio that Paris had fallen; and all the German officers stood up and started singing the Horst Wessel song and the German national anthem, and raising their arms in the Nazi salute. The student, Bethge, was astonished to see Bonhoeffer, his principal, also standing and saluting, and lustily joining in the singing. 'Put up your arm,' whispered Bonhoeffer to Bethge. 'This thing isn't worth dying for,' he said, pointing to his arm.

In fact, Bonhoeffer died within five years. He gave his life for what he believed. But, in 1940, his time had not yet come. He was following his Master, who had to work out his mysticism in the politics of his day: politics that involved the High Priests in Jerusalem, a Roman Governor Pilate, a local ruler Herod, and the voice of the people.

Bonhoeffer and Jesus both had to work out what was expedient. 'It is expedient for you . . .' said Jesus on one occasion. There was a time for him to speak and a time to be silent.

It's laughable to think that followers of Jesus in any generation can avoid working out in politics what they believe. Mystique has to be translated into politique.

———— • ◆ • ————

44

The wrecks of time

Saturday 28 June 1997

What is happening in Hong Kong this weekend involves a surprising number of us, and involves us at varying levels.

It was over 40 years ago that I was offered a job in Hong Kong, at the Anglican Cathedral. For various reasons, the job fell through; but when, twenty years later, I fetched up there again for a couple of weeks, and was again asked to consider a job there, which I eventually refused, I knew I'd never be able to forget either the place or its people.

Like many this weekend, I'm anxious for the future of Hong Kong – not just in an abstract way. I know individuals who've had to decide whether to stay there or get out; and others who couldn't leave even if they wanted to; and others who are leaving reluctantly and painfully – leaving friends and family; and yet others who are glad to be staying.

And here in Britain, however pro- or anti-Empire we've been – and I can still remember as a child, waving a Union Jack on Empire Day – we know that the complex Empire connection, whatever it was, for good or ill, is being cut this weekend.

Two hundred years ago, a man was born in Exeter called John Bowring. On leaving school, he entered a merchant's office. In 1824 he became the first editor of the radical *Westminster Review*, and sat in Parliament from 1825 to 1849. That year, he became British Consul in Hong Kong. In 1854 he was knighted, and made Governor. In 1856, after an incident involving an insult to the British flag, Bowring ordered the bombardment of Canton. Such was the roughness of our Empire's history – indeed, the roughness of our human history. But there's one thing more we might well remember about Sir John Bowring on this particular day. He wrote poems, at least one of which you will still find in our hymn books. He wrote:

> In the Cross of Christ I glory
> > Towering o'er the wrecks of time
> All the light of sacred story
> > Gathers round its head sublime.

Today is an appropriate day, surely, for reflecting on that powerful phrase 'the wrecks of time', and for reflecting whether – and how – God is in Hong Kong's history, and ours; and, indeed, where the Cross of Christ is to be found not only within that history but towering over it.

It's not difficult, of course, simply to dismiss John Bowring as a child of his time; but that still leaves us with the mystery of the meaning of history, of Hong Kong's and our own.

45

Corruption

Saturday 5 July 1997

Corruption in any society is rightly treated seriously – especially the corruption of those who aspire to and accept high office, whether that office be one to which people are elected, as in the case of MPs, or one at which they arrived by inheritance, as in the case of what we still call the nobility and royalty.

I remember, ages ago, when I was a student, the Dean of my College saying to me: 'Eric, you're a romantic, and unless you have a high doctrine of corruption – corruption in church as well as state – you'll not survive.' To be honest, in those days of my youth, I didn't really know what he was getting at. It needed another 25 years of experience before I did, and then it was particularly painful, because it was corruption in the Church that I had to experience and confront.

It's no good pretending that to take corruption seriously is simple: either the exposing of it when and where it needs to be exposed, or the remedying of it. Doing justly by the guilty and showing mercy are both important but often difficult. There's a cheap attitude to corruption which passes over and pardons too easily. One of the prophets talked of 'healing the sins of my people lightly'. And there's another cheap attitude to corruption which almost delights in smelling out sleaze and scandal in others – 'muck-raking' we call it. The newspapers make a good deal of money out of it; and self-righteous people thrive on it.

The German theologian, Dietrich Bonhoeffer, who was executed in a Nazi concentration camp, talked of 'cheap grace'. He knew from his own bitter experience both the extent and depth of his nation's corruption and the cost of any profound forgiveness.

Not simply in the end but right from the beginning we need to face the fact that corruption is not something that only affects *other* people: it's something that's at the very centre of ourselves, of all of us.

Judgement needs to begin with ourselves; so, too, does mercy – our understanding of mercy, redemption and forgiveness. And then we'll be able to minister to others.

We constituents need to understand our corruption, and our need of justice and mercy, if we're to expect it and exact it from our MPs, and be equipped to show it to them.

46

Why are we waiting?

Saturday 12 July 1997

A few nights ago, I went to a new production of *Waiting for Godot* at the Old Vic. Peter Hall — now Sir Peter Hall — directed the first English production, in 1955, and he's directing this latest production, 42 years on.

When *Waiting for Godot* was first produced, waves of hostility came across the footlights, and the mass exodus of the audience, which was to characterize the first weeks of the production, started soon after the curtain went up. It was Harold Hobson, then the theatre critic of the *Sunday Times* who had the courage to tell his readers they must go and see the play, and started to reverse the public's attitude. Ralph Richardson wrote that in turning down the invitation to play a major part in the play he had turned down the greatest play of his lifetime.

The play, in a nutshell, is a parable of human existence, with Vladimir and Estragon, two tramps, the main characters, representing the human condition of just 'being there'. Samuel Beckett, the Irishman who wrote the play, said Godot is simply the person for whom the tramps wait. Hope, fear, despair, renewed expectation, uncertainty, charity and compassion, are all there with them. And there's humour in the play: the pathetic humour we associate with Charlie Chaplin, and Laurel and Hardy.

At one point in the play I wanted to sing out, 'Why are we waiting?'; but the answer was in fact obvious — because Godot hasn't yet come. So the tramps wait, and go on waiting.

There are a lot of people in the world at the moment who are waiting for something to turn up. Godot for them is the unknown and unknowable future. And that may be in the hands of the Chinese Government, or someone locally who controls old people's housing. But the condition of such people is no different – eventually and essentially – from our own. The human condition itself – and this is the point of the play – is that of waiting for an unknown future. As a Christian, that future, I believe, to be in the hands of a loving God no matter what events unfold – including, of course, suffering and death.

The more dreamy of the two tramps in the play behaves as if he were actually involved in the crucifixion – not just thinking about it. And that's about as profoundly religious a way of conceiving the existence of all of us as there could possibly be in this so often lunatic world.

———— ◆ ————

47

Alone on a wide, wide sea

Saturday 11 October 1997

Many people have been keeping this week as National Poetry Week. *Poetry Please!* has become a particularly popular programme on radio recently.

The poem I'd most want to hear just now is 'The Rime of the Ancient Mariner'. It was 200 years ago – to the month – that Samuel Taylor Coleridge began to plan the poem. His friend, William Wordsworth, had pointed out a passage in a book he'd been reading: Captain Shelvocke's *A Voyage Round the World by Way of the Great South Sea*. He tells how the melancholy second captain killed an albatross when their ship was attempting to get round Cape Horn to the Pacific. But why and how Coleridge should, from that passage, conjure one of the most musical and haunting poems in the English language, is a mystery.

I don't suppose many of us now can recite much of 'The Ancient Mariner', but most of us know some of its lines: the curious beginning, when the mariner stops a wedding guest, and won't let him go till he's told his story:

> It is an ancient mariner
> And he stoppeth one of three.
>
> 'By thy long grey beard and glittering eye,
> Now wherefore stopp'st thou me?
>
> The Bridegroom's doors are open'd wide,
> And I am next of kin'.

But he does stop him – as I suspect he'll stop us, once we start reading the poem.

I love the lines that describe the stillness of the ship at sea:

> nor breath nor motion
> As idle as a painted ship
> Upon a painted ocean.

And, of course, we all love:

> Water, water, every where,
> And all the boards did shrink;
> Water, water, every where
> Nor any drop to drink.

But the poem isn't only a rattling good yarn. The killing of the albatross reminds us all of the sanctity of the natural world. Sun, moon, stars, lightning, sea: they have for all of us at times a terrible power. Coleridge describes a cosmos of which man is not at the centre; and he wonderfully depicts a loneliness at sea which those of us who live in cities can often forget:

> Alone on a wide wide sea!

But at the end of the poem are four remarkable lines which speak of what Albert Schweitzer called 'reverence for life':

> He prayeth best, who loveth best
> All things both great and small.
> For the dear God who loveth us,
> He made, and loveth all.

———◆———

48

Redundant

Saturday 18 October 1997

It's more than ten years now since I spent much of my time working with the Archbishop's Commission on Urban Priority Areas – which produced the report *Faith in the City* – which would be heard all round the country, not least in Parliament. In the intervening years, I've tried to keep in touch with the areas I visited with the Commission, to see whether the report was having any lasting effects. Today, I'm going up to County Durham, to visit a parish on the coast where the vicar is moving on to new work, after eight years of hard but rewarding work there.

Parish magazines are often laughed at, but I shall never forget the Vicar's Letter in that parish magazine which I read on one of my last visits to the parish, and decided to keep. Here's part of what the vicar wrote:

When I came to Seaham, in 1989, the three collieries of the town were still working full shifts and flat out. Within five years, all three had closed down, and their winding shafts and surface buildings wiped from the face of the earth. However, even in 1989 men were being retired early, at the age of fifty.

Although they received large redundancy payments, [and the vicar asked us to note that word] they felt unwanted, and had lost the only social standing they had in the community. 'He's a miner at Dawdon,' people would say, or 'at Vane Tempest' or at '*The* Colliery, Seaham'. People were proud to be miners, and the loss of this status was too much for some to live with. Some drank themselves to death, others took their lives by more instant means: the deep waters of the sea, the rope and the overdose. In three years I had conducted the funerals of more suicides than in the previous twenty-five years of my ministry. But others adapted well to leisure and retirement, and the three churches of my parish would not now survive without the voluntary help of such people.

Of course, in eight years, the vicar hasn't been able to alter the employment situation in that parish. That's not been his primary job – though there are individuals whom he has been able to see get appropriate training for work.

Much of the work of the clergy isn't easy to define; but I know this weekend I shall meet many people in that parish who will say they're thankful for the work of their parish priest. He's renewed their ability to be hopeful, their capacity to care for one another, their sense of belonging to one another; but, above all, their sense of purpose in life.

And people with such gifts can never be 'redundant'.

———— •◆• ————

49

The dial hand of Time

Saturday 25 October 1997

I expect you've made a note to put your clocks back tonight. I always think it's rather an eerie moment, because most of the time we think we know exactly where we are with Time, then suddenly we find we don't.

Most of the time, of course, we take Time for granted, and rarely reflect on its mystery. Because we can count seconds, minutes, hours, days, months, years – we almost come to think we know all about Time. And then, suddenly, something happens that jolts us into the middle of its mystery – say, the untimely death of a friend. Or something much more mundane: we mislay our watch. 'I'm lost without it,' we say. Nowadays we're often the slaves of time.

Shakespeare seems to me to have thought more about Time than almost any of us. He speaks of the 'dial hand' of a clock, the movement of which is imperceptible, yet Time goes by. He refers to 'Old Time, the clock-setter, that bald sexton, Time.' He says, with great conviction, 'Love's not Time's fool'; but he also says, with painful realism: 'Time will come and take my Love away.'

The mystery of Time is, in part, the fact that it's the very stage on which our life is lived: the very stuff and raw material of life. But in time it will vanish away – or, rather, in time we shall vanish. We can either treat that as a threat – perhaps a terrifying threat – or we can see time as one of God's greatest gifts from his inexhaustible store of Love.

I'm not, of course, suggesting that that attitude to time is gained in a second. I've already suggested it may be the pain of some sudden bereavement which makes us reflect on the mystery of Time. Neither am I one of those who will quote – as though it's always true – 'Time, the great Healer'. Sometimes our wounds seem never to heal.

There's something to be said for the couplet of the Victorian poet Henry Dobson:

Time goes, you say? Ah no!
Alas, Time stays, we go.

Yet I prefer to think that the Loving Creator of Time stays; and when we go from Time we go only further into his Love. And nothing shall separate us from that Love.

———— •◆• ————

50

An awful responsibility

Saturday 1 November 1997

Until a few months ago, I was, for nearly twenty years, what is called 'Preacher to Gray's Inn': a task which involved not only preaching to judges – and their wives and families – not only speaking to them, but listening to them and sharing meals with them, in their homes and in Gray's Inn itself. When I asked a judge – as I often did – 'What have you been doing lately?', on many occasions I received, not a brief answer, but, as likely as not, the details of a case of great complexity; and, not seldom, the sharing of an agony caused not only by complex and conflicting evidence but understanding of opposing sides.

My first Dean of Chapel was Lord Edmund Davies – alas, dead now for four years – who meted out severe sentences to those involved in the Great Train Robbery. I can't tell you how many times he went over that case with me – still, in his retirement, reflecting on the pros and cons of the sentences he gave on that occasion.

The American system of justice is, of course, considerably different from our own, but when I heard the Court's decision yesterday, in the case of Louise Woodward, my heart went out to all the parties in that tragic case: the parents of the child – that nineteen-year-old *au pair* – who speaks, surely, to us all of the rights and wrongs of leaving such an untrained person in charge of an eight-month-old baby. My heart went out as well to the defending and prosecuting counsel, to the judge, and to the eleven members of the jury, burdened with such awful responsibility.

Sometimes, when we speak of 'justice', we think of some figure, like the statue that tops the Old Bailey; and it's right we should have an idea and ideal of justice which is utterly independent. Yet, in the end, justice inescapably depends on fallible human judgement and wisdom, and what we human beings think and feel and say about one another, and the regard we have for the truth.

Pontius Pilate is remembered for ever for his question, 'What is truth?' In the Louise Woodward case we now know an appeal by the defence against the verdict is likely to be lodged.

Whatever else we've learnt this last week, we learnt again that we are all human beings with a capacity for concern for truth, and with a responsibility for truth. God help all those who will still be involved in the Woodward case. God help us all in our concern and responsibility for truth. And on this All Saints and All Souls weekend, may God, in his love and mercy, take care of Matthew, the baby of that tormented family.

———————•◆•———————

51

What lies beyond

Saturday 24 January 1998

It's only 24 days since we were all saying to one another: 'Happy New Year'; but, in those three weeks or so, I've had to help with the funerals of four friends of mine. They were all getting on in years, and some might say the life of each of them had virtually run its course – though it was some form of cancer which brought to an end three of those lives.

I was privileged to be at the bedside of two of those friends of mine only a few hours before they died, and said prayers with them; and they both died at peace, free from fear and anxiety. One of them was, in fact, longing to die, and could hardy wait to be released. She looked forward to what she explicitly called 'Heaven', and to seeing her husband again, who'd been an eminent medical professor, whose funeral I'd helped with two years ago.

This sudden harvest of deaths has brought back to my mind a question which my father asked me on the day my mother died. Both of them were in their eighties. My father had been a business-man, and didn't often ask me religious questions; but on this particular day he asked a question which was like a shriek of pain. He suddenly blurted out: 'Eric, you're a priest. Can you tell me why God – if he's a God of Love – allows you to come close to someone for years and years, only to rip them away from you when you most need them?'

It wasn't a question to which there was an easy answer. And I remember first thanking him for asking me such a real and heartfelt question. I could have said – as some do – 'Aren't the years of hap-piness you've had together something worth having in themselves?' But I knew that wouldn't have gone to the heart of the matter, and dealt with the pain my father was understandably feeling at the time. I remembered St Paul's saying: 'If we have hope only in this world we are of all men most miserable.' So I said to my father: 'The Chris-tian hope isn't that you've seen the last of mother. Jesus said to his disciples: "I go to prepare a place for you"'. 'Yes,' Dad said, and then sat there silent with his thoughts.

I realize that not least the busy-ness of our modern secular world doesn't really encourage most of us to face such questions these days, until – like me this month, and like my father at the time of my mother's death – death stares us in the face. But I think, in fact, it would help most people to give some thought to what lies beyond this world before they're *forced* to think about it.

———•◆•———

52

The exact help needed

Saturday 31 January 1998

At the end of this week, in which the fiftieth anniversary of the death of the great political and spiritual Indian leader, Mahatma Gandhi, has been celebrated, it's appropriate, I think, to spare a thought for one of the greatest influences in his life: the English priest, C. F. Andrews.

'Charlie' Andrews was born in Newcastle in 1871. At Pembroke College, Cambridge, he won the Burney Prize with an essay on 'The Relation of Christianity to the Conflict between Capital and Labour'. His greatest friend at Cambridge was Basil Westcott, the son of the then Bishop of Durham. He recorded the Bishop saying to him one day: 'Remember, Andrews, nothing nothing that is truly human can be left outside the Christian faith.'

After getting a First at Cambridge, he worked as a layman in a Sunderland shipyard parish; then, after ordination, he took charge of the Pembroke College Mission in South London, near the Elephant and Castle.

When he heard the news that his friend Basil Westcott had died of cholera in India, he felt he must, literally, take his place; and in 1904 he went out there. He soon saw that Christianity and Hinduism *had* to be friends. He became a great and lifelong friend of the Indian poet, Rabindranath Tagore.

In 1914, he heard that in South Africa, in Natal, Indians had been fired on, and decided to go there immediately. It was there that he first met Gandhi. He describes in his diary an evening with Gandhi in Durban that ended with the singing of hymns both in English and Gujerati. It was Gandhi who asked for the hymn written by Cardinal Newman: 'Lead, kindly light . . .'. Within the next ten years, Andrews' friendship became central to Gandhi's life. There's a lovely letter from Gandhi to Andrews of 20 October 1924, in which Gandhi writes: 'I have missed you all today. O your love.'

Andrews spent much time in various parts of the world where Indian workers were in trouble. I've seen tributes to his work in Fiji, Uganda and the West Indies. I can't forget his tombstone in Calcutta, which has on it the words 'Deenabandhu: Friend of the Poor'.

The saying of Charles Freer Andrews that I like most of all concerns charity: 'Charity,' he said 'is the careful enquiry into the needs of others that enables one to give the exact help needed.'

———— •◆• ————

53

Truth and the Titanic

Saturday 7 February 1998

One evening this week I went to see the film *Titanic*. I hadn't seen one of the largest London cinemas so packed for a long time.

I had a particular reason for wanting to see the film. When I was a young teenager, with already a love for music, one of the best singers in our locality was a survivor of the *Titanic* – by name: Eva Hart. I remember her singing the soprano solos in Mendelssohn's *Elijah*; but I also remember the awe with which people spoke of her, because she had so narrowly survived that terrible disaster at sea, 25 years earlier. She was only seven when she was taken by her parents on the *Titanic*'s maiden voyage, to emigrate to Canada. Her father had said to her, as the lifeboat was lowered: 'Stay with your mother, and hold her hand tightly, like a good girl.' That was the last she saw or heard of him. She tells the heart-rending story in her published autobiography, a signed copy of which I've treasured for years.

I didn't expect to *enjoy* the film. How can you possibly enjoy a film about a disaster, in which more than 1,500 lives were lost? But neither did I expect to come out of the film *angry* – which I did: because at the very heart and centre of the film is a fiction, a relationship of fantasy. It's as if the true story – the story of people like Eva Hart – was not enough. The film had to be turned into a romance that crosses the barriers of class – on board ship, the barriers between first class and steerage.

One of the chief casualties in the film is therefore truth itself.

We've most of us heard sound-bites like: 'More money was spent on this film than on any other.' And we've probably heard that 'So many have now seen the film, that the money spent has already been recovered.' The suggestion is that the money made justifies the money spent.

There are many events these days when truth is literally 'up for sale': when tragedy, personal and social, virtually becomes entertainment, via, say, the tabloids.

I know that T. S. Eliot said:

> Human kind
> Cannot bear very much reality.

But it's also important for our human survival that we have reverence for truth. And, when any part of our life is centred on falsehood, something of our true humanity drowns.

———— • ◆ • ————

54

Companions

Saturday 18 April 1998

Just before Easter, I went to a gathering in London that had been called to publicize the work of a charity named Emmaus. It's part of an international movement of nearly 400 small communities, all of them providing a place where homeless men and women can live and work. They call each other 'companions', because the original meaning of the word is, literally, 'people who share bread together'.

A few days after Easter, I wandered into the National Gallery in London. There, in Room 32, I was confronted by Caravaggio's great painting of the Risen Christ at Supper – at Emmaus. It's not surprising that so many artists should have found the subject so fascinating. Rembrandt returns to it repeatedly: in etchings, drawings and paintings.

The story itself is a painting in words. Two disciples, on the road to Emmaus, are joined by a stranger; but it's when they reach Emmaus that they recognize the stranger as the Risen Christ: when they sit at table together, and he takes bread, and blesses it, and shares it.

It's marvellous the way Caravaggio portrays one of the disciples as so astounded at what he sees that he almost jumps out of his chair. He grips the armrests with both hands, and sticks his head a long way forward. Clearly, he can hardly believe his eyes! The other disciple, equally astonished and incredulous, spreads his arms out wide.

But there's another figure in the painting, watching what's going on – the landlord. I wondered what he made of the Risen Christ? Did he recognize something different about him? Did they have much to say to each other? It was the landlord – who provided the meal for Jesus and the disciples – who made me say to myself: 'That word "companion" has something to say to us all. We're all companions – the disciples, the landlord, Jesus, the homeless and those with homes. We're all "members one of another": we share a common humanity.'

Perhaps one of the most important and Christ-like moments of recognition in life is when we can simply say, in Shakespeare's words:

> I live with bread like you
> Taste grief
> Need friends.

55

Trevor Huddleston RIP

Tuesday 21 April 1998

Ten years ago, Archbishop Trevor Huddleston, who died yesterday, asked me to write his life. As I discussed his life with him, we became close friends. One day, I found myself asking myself: 'What was the crucial event in his life?' When I'd decided, I asked him whether I'd got it right. His enthusiastically approved of my choice.

It was a Sunday in 1953, in Sophiatown, one of the black townships of Johannesburg. The authorities had suddenly decided to bulldoze all the housing. A protest meeting was hastily arranged for that Sunday in the local cinema. Fr Huddleston, as he then was, as soon as his service in the Church of Christ the King was over, hurried to the cinema. Already, a thousand people were inside and an even larger crowd outside. Trevor found the South African CID there arguing that they should be allowed in. He phoned a friendly QC, who told him they had no right to be there, and Trevor requested them to leave.

Just after he had finished addressing the meeting, the entrance door of the cinema burst open, and a body of police marched up the centre aisle and arrested one of the local leaders. Outraged, the people rose to their feet. Trevor was aware of the acute danger of the situation. He knew he must deal with the police; but at the door of the cinema he was confronted by a policeman with a tommy-gun at the ready. The people inside could have rushed the door and there would have been a massacre. Huddleston said to the police officer: 'If you call off the police, I will see that the meeting ends peacefully'; but the officer threatened him with arrest. Outside the cinema they tried also to arrest the 35- year-old Nelson Mandela, who had only just been released from his sentence. Trevor told the police they had no legal right to arrest Mandela again.

Huddleston's action that day was decisive. He'd not only saved Mandela from prison – for the time being – he'd averted a massacre. When the full story of Trevor Huddleston comes to be written, it will be acts of extraordinary courage like that for which he will be remembered.

He was later Bishop of Masasi in Central Africa, Bishop of Stepney, here in London, and Archbishop of the Indian Ocean. But his greatest work will undoubtedly be seen to be his work for and alongside the black and coloured peoples of South Africa. I have realized lately that many people under 40 don't even know who Trevor Huddleston was. Certainly all his titles will mean nothing. Yet President Mandela has said simply: 'No white person has done more for South Africa than Trevor Huddleston.' No more need now be said, except: 'For Trevor Huddleston, thank God.'

———— •◆• ————

56

The Community of the Resurrection

Saturday 2 May 1998

Last Sunday, I went back to the parish where I was vicar nearly 40 years ago – St George's, Camberwell, in inner South London. The building I knew as 'St George's' is now a block of flats; but there's a new church and community centre combined. It's as though the old 1820s St George's was the tomb from which the new St George's has risen.

Very many of the people I worshipped with in the years 1959 to

1964, are now, of course, dead; but as I returned there, they filled my mind and heart.

Last Tuesday, I had to go up to Yorkshire, for the funeral of Bishop Trevor Huddleston, who was a member of what's marvellously called 'The Community of the Resurrection'. On Thursday, I attended the funeral of another friend. So this week – very appropriately, only three weeks after Easter – I've been thinking a lot about those I love but see no longer.

Many people say, 'When you're dead, you're dead.' As a Christian, I don't myself believe that. I have to admit that what will happen when I die – and what has happened to those I love but see no longer – is beyond all words. I can't describe it. But I can say that the love which Jesus revealed God to be has in store for us new life beyond the grave. So I don't just think of a computerized list of those who've died. They're still part of our company: our companions on the way. We're one communion and fellowship – one family. That title of Bishop Huddleston's community, 'The Community of the Resurrection', seems to me to fit exactly the community I belong to now, and will go on belonging to when I die.

At the beginning of Trevor Huddleston's funeral, in his community's large church, the organist played first of all the rather astringent *Prelude* and *Fugue in B minor* of Bach. It had a hint of sternness and judgement about it. But then he was inspired to play Bach's much-loved chorale prelude 'Sheep may safely graze'. It was a wonderful Easter image of heaven in music.

St Paul said: 'If we have hope only in this life we are of all people most miserable.' And there's a prayer which begins: 'God, you have prepared for those who love you such good things as pass our understanding.' In that lovely phrase, it seems to me, faith, hope and love have been most marvellously combined.

———•◆•———

57

Harmony

Saturday 4 July 1998

One evening this week, I went to visit a school in the East End of London, in Bethnal Green. I suppose there's nothing more what we call 'inner city' these days than that area. And I've no doubt that in that comprehensive school I was visiting, the problems for teachers and for parents – not to mention the children – are often daunting beyond words. But that evening was for me, and for all of us who were lucky enough to be there, one of sheer delight.

We had gathered for a concert that was being given to celebrate the opening of the new performing arts department of the school. We were entertained by the school orchestra and the school jazz band, and there were several solo items. There were trumpets, flutes, violins, drums – and 'Cockles and Mussels' played as a trombone solo. There was classical music and the blues.

I'd been asked there to see and hear my 13-year-old godson play the saxophone. But what struck me above all was the way in which all the performers supported each other, and how the audience – mainly, of course, parents – responded with enthusiasm to each item.

The news this week has had much in it which I've found very depressing, because it has revealed again how difficult we human beings find it to live together in unity. I'm thinking particularly of what happened at the Lawrence inquiry at the Elephant and Castle, round the corner from where I live. Then there was the murder trial of Billy Jo Jenkins' killer, and the very fragile peace in Northern Ireland.

But that comprehensive school I was visiting – which was probably racially, and therefore religiously, as comprehensive as one could find anywhere in Britain today – renewed in me hope. Here was a diverse group of young people enjoying each other's company; learning not only to live, literally, in harmony, but to respect one another's different contributions.

When Shakespeare said that music was 'the food of love', he was saying something profoundly spiritual. Making music together can teach us something about love and about human belonging. It can teach us that all of us in the human family are meant to play in the human orchestra, and that we can make a joyful and lively and lovely sound together when we give our hearts and minds to it.

So, this morning, I simply want to thank God for all that teachers, parents, children and schools are doing together to bring harmony to our complex and often conflicting world.

58

Compromise

Saturday 11 July 1998

For the whole of this week, two words – confrontation *and* compromise, confrontation *or* compromise – have been ringing in our ears.

Most of us are not living in Northern Ireland, so the anxious question for us is: 'Will they – either side – compromise?' But if you're living in Northern Ireland that anxiety, for many, will now be at fever pitch.

What does the word 'compromise' mean? Well, the *Shorter Oxford Dictionary* says it means 'to adjust or settle differences between parties: 1798; To settle by mutual concession: 1672. The joint promise or agreement made by contending parties to abide by the decision of an arbiter; Partial surrender of one's position for the sake of coming to terms: 1516.' I've quoted the dates against those definitions, because, for me, they underline the fact that human beings have been faced with the question of compromise for centuries.

Edmund Burke, the eighteenth-century Anglo-Irish statesman and political philosopher, said: 'All government, indeed, every human benefit and enjoyment, every virtue and every prudent act, is founded on compromise and barter.' That's quite a thought-provoking claim – though, surely, it claims too much. And exaggeration is no help at such a time and in a such a situation.

This week, the sculpted figures of ten twentieth-century martyrs have been placed in niches on the facade of Westminster Abbey. You don't immediately think of compromise and martyrs in the same breath. You associate martyrs with that other word, confrontation – though one of my favourite stories of Dietrich Bonhoeffer, one of those ten martyrs, is of his giving the Nazi salute on one occasion, though a very few years later he would be giving his life. There was a time to do one thing and a time to do the other.

Christians have constantly to remind themselves that Jesus gave his life. In a sense, he was the first Christian martyr; but his example of confrontation was certainly not one of violence. Yet, this morning, it would be little help to anyone to think that in two and a half minutes or so one could come up with a profound solution to a particular situation with which others have wrestled for a week – indeed, for weeks, and months, and years.

Perhaps all that is to be said this morning is that there is certainly no shame in the way of compromise-through-arbitration; and everything to be said for thinking again of the example of Jesus – whichever our particular 'side' happens to be.

59

Bring my soul out of prison

Saturday 18 July 1998

Nelson Mandela was born 80 years ago today. He's surely one of the greatest people of our age. The human race is the better for his presence among us.

I've only myself met him once. It was Easter Day, 1990: the day he arrived on his first visit to England, after his release from prison. I shan't forget that day. I was preaching that afternoon in Westminster Abbey. In the evening, I had to represent the charity Christian Action of which I was then Director, at a reception for Mandela. It was Canon Collins, the founder of Christian Action, who had done so much to organize the legal defence of people like Mandela, unjustly imprisoned in South Africa, and to help the dependants of those in prison.

It was curious that at Evensong in the Abbey there seemed to be so many references to Easter which also had something to say about Mandela. There was, I remember, a verse in the Psalm for the day which said: 'Bring my soul out of prison.' The familiar Easter hymns frequently rhymed 'risen' and 'prison', so that Mandela's release seemed part of the continuing Easter story.

And that was no surprise. John Bunyan had written in the seventeenth century:

> For though men hold my outward man
> > Within their bolts and bars
> Yet by the faith of Christ I can
> > Rise upward to the stars.

One of my favourite books is an anthology gathered by Lady Elizabeth Basset, one of the ladies-in-waiting to the Queen Mother. She called it *Each in His Prison*. The whole book consists of writings by people who have triumphed in different kinds of captivity. It's a celebration of the human spirit's capacity to transcend suffering, not least imprisonment: to rise above it, and make of it a creative rather than a destructive experience.

When I met Nelson Mandela that Easter Day, I felt I was meeting someone for whom the prayer, 'Bring my soul out of prison', had been most marvellously answered.

To celebrate his eightieth birthday, I doubt whether we could do anything better than remember – in any way that is open to us – those who are still unjustly imprisoned, not least in the labyrinth of their own mind.

'Bring my soul out of prison' is a good prayer for us all, as we think thankfully, on his birthday, of Nelson Mandela's example to us.

60

Doing the Resurrection

Saturday 25 July 1998

John Mortimer, in his novel, *Summer's Lease*, describes some tourists in Tuscany having an early breakfast, so that they can 'do the Resurrection before lunch'.

I had a four-day break this week and followed in those tourists' footsteps. Some kind friends of mine had taken a fortnight's lease of a house outside the little town of San Sepolchro in Tuscany, and we 'did the Resurrection before lunch'. It's a painting by the fifteenth century artist Piero della Francesca – which Aldous Huxley, in a marvellous essay, simply calls 'the best picture':

> When at last one has arrived at San Sepolchro, what is to be seen? A little town surrounded by walls, set in a broad flat valley between hills . . . a not very interesting church, and, finally, the best picture in the world – painted in fresco, on the wall of a room in the town hall.

I saw that painting last Tuesday. I've been longing to see it for years. Piero has painted Christ at the very moment of the Resurrection. He's stepping out of the sepulchre – one foot in the grave, the other on the edge of the altar-like tomb. He's as upright as the staff of the banner he's holding in his right hand. He's the very embodiment of life and power. His piercing eyes look straight at you – almost *through* you. Although those guarding the tomb are unaware of what's happened – they're fast asleep! – nature has already begun to awake. The trees on the left of the painting are still dead; but those on the right are green with new life.

As I say, it's a fifteenth-century painting, and you wonder what would be the equivalent today. In fact, earlier this year, the artist Matthew Browne scandalized many by doing a kind of satire of this very painting, with the footballer Eric Cantona in the place of Christ, as if to say: 'Football now occupies the time and place – in England as well as Italy – that religion occupied for most people in Tuscany in the fifteenth century.'

But football can't attempt to deal with what happens when disaster hits you – like, say, the New Guinea earthquake – nor can it give a reason for our existence, not least for artists like Piero, however absorbing and exciting a part of life it can provide.

But each of us in this life has to discover for ourselves sometime – with our own thoughts and experience and gifts – what Piero, with such compelling conviction, put into his painting of the Resurrection over 500 years ago.

—— •◆• ——

61

Our precarious existence

Saturday 1 August 1998

This week, I was privileged to preach at the memorial service for an 80-year-old friend of mine, who'd been an officer in the Iniskilling Dragoon Guards. Early in May 1940, only days before Dunkirk, he'd been reported dead. Then, on 18 May that year, the War Office revised that to 'Missing, believed killed in action', which was followed by a letter of confirmation. Then, on 2 June, another wire from the War Office corrected that to 'Killed in action', with yet another letter of confirmation, two days later. His mother put an obituary notice in *The Times*. She received a letter of condolence from the King; and other letters poured in, which she answered. Then, on 19 June, she got a rather apologetic letter from the War Office, going back to 'Missing, believed killed in action'. Not until 5 August 1940, did my friend's mother receive the news – which she could hardly dare to believe or tell anyone about – that her son was in fact alive in Brussels; wounded, but recovering well.

He was, for the next four years, a prisoner of war. He lived the rest of his life to the full – with one of his legs amputated below the knee, after the wounds he'd received – until his death this year.

When I prepared the address for the memorial service to Michael – to give him his name – I was overwhelmed by a sense of 'most of his life might never have happened': his marriage, his children, his friendships, the jobs he did in the War Office after the war, and in civilian life. It could all so easily have been prevented by the shell that hit his tank in 1940. Had Michael died then, I myself would, of course, never have known him, or been able to give that address at his memorial service.

As I mused on Michael's life, I was overcome by a sense of the precariousness of all our lives: fertilization and birth, and then survival – in my case, for over 70 years now – all could so easily not have happened. And the people one has met, like Michael, one could so easily have missed meeting; and yet some of those meetings have made, as they say, 'all the difference'.

An important part of religion, I believe, is wonder at our very existence – our precarious existence – combined with trust in the Love of God, who, in the 'changes and chances of this fleeting world', has us 'fast', as Newman says, 'within his ample palm'.

———— • ◆ • ————

62

No thought of the harvest

Saturday 26 September 1998

It's nearly 60 years since I first read any of the poetry of T. S. Eliot, whose birthday it is today. I can still remember going into a bookshop in Gracechurch Street in the City, when I was a 15-year-old, at work, then, as an office boy, at a riverside wharf on the Thames. I picked up Eliot's long poem, 'East Coker', which had just been published separately, for a shilling, that month: September 1940 – the very month that I watched one of our wharves by London Bridge blazing furiously after a night air-raid. That poem – which I can't pretend I fully understood at the time – fed me with phrases which have kept me going all these years. The very first words: 'In my beginning is my end'. And, a little later: 'I said to my soul, be still, and wait without hope . . . The faith and the love and the hope are all in the waiting.'

In September 1940, in the middle of the blitz in the first years of the war, there was a lot of waiting to be done. But that poem, as I say, has gone on feeding me. One of its best lines is particularly powerful for me today – now I'm 73: 'Old men ought to be explorers'.

'East Coker' was the first of Eliot's *Four Quartets* as he called them. I could hardly wait for them to be published. The second, 'Burnt Norton', I bought – again for a shilling, at the same bookshop – in February 1941; and the third, 'The Dry Salvages', in September that year; and the last of the four, 'Little Gidding', in 1942: the year that Singapore surrendered to the Japanese. I still treasure those first editions: four shillings for the lot, but worth their weight in gold.

'Little Gidding' perhaps means most to me now. It quotes from St Julian of Norwich:

> And all shall be well
> And all manner of thing shall be well.

And it has this marvellous passage:

> With the drawing of this Love and the
>   voice of this Calling
> We shall not cease from exploration
> And the end of all our exploring
> Will be to arrive where we started
> And know the place for the first time.

Eliot was a very private person. He looked like a businessman. He was a very devout Christian – churchwarden of St Stephen's Church, Gloucester Road in West London – but went through some dark times himself, from which I suspect he quarried two of his lines which come to my rescue time and time again:

> Take no thought of the harvest
> But only of proper sowing.

63

Jesus the entertainer

Saturday 3 October 1998

The *New Statesman* has a column 'This England', which usually knocks something or someone. This week it knocks a Staffordshire vicar, the vicar of Burslem, who has installed a bar at the back of his church. It illustrates its story with a crucifix and a crucified Christ holding a pint pot.

Now it's easy to knock that vicar, Robert Johnson, but I think he has a lot in the Gospels on his side. Jesus was derided by the Pharisees because of the people he ate and drank with. 'Why do you eat and drink with publicans and sinners?' they asked. I don't think that vicar would be derided by Jesus. I don't suppose he'll get Five Thousand in his bar; but I can see Jesus welcoming and blessing those who do go there; and I can even see him taking a turn behind the bar. 'I'm here,' he'd say, 'as a servant.'

It was Jesus who said to Zacchaeus, the taxman: 'Can I come and have a meal with you?' And no doubt the meal included a drink.

Once, Jesus was having a meal when a woman of doubtful reputation came in off the streets and poured quite costly perfume on him. His host was clearly embarrassed; but Jesus wasn't. And I can't see him being embarrassed by a bar in Burslem.

The Last Supper, whatever else it was, was a meal. Jesus entertained his friends and followers to bread and wine – and food for thought – and, above all, with who he was. I suspect that Upper Room and a bar at the back of a church have a good deal in common.

Maybe there are others who, with the *New Statesman*, find all this uncongenial. But time and again, St Paul writes to the first Christians: 'Be given to hospitality'; 'Use hospitality'; 'Be a lover of hospitality.' 'Receive one another,' he writes, 'as Christ received you, to the glory of God the Father.' 'Entertain one another' he might have written, 'as Christ entertained you . . .' I imagine that's exactly what the Vicar of Burslem had in mind.

Of course, there's a time and a place for everything: a time for worship and a time for the bar at the back of the church. I can see

Jesus entertaining people with his stories at the bar rather than from the pulpit. As far as I know, no one's yet written a book called *Jesus the Entertainer*, but it's about time they did. It's a profoundly entertaining subject.

64

Welfare

Saturday 10 October 1998

The political party conference season is at an end; but the problems the political parties must address are still with us.

I've been reading a book – published in the last fortnight – by Frank Field, erstwhile Minister for Welfare Reform. Not surprisingly, he calls it *Reflections on Welfare Reform*. I can mention the book on *Thought for the Day*, since it isn't a book that belongs to Frank Field's party. One of the lectures is, indeed, a tribute to the Conservative politician, Sir Keith Joseph; and another, to the great Liberal, Lord Beveridge.

Frank Field writes unashamedly as a Christian in politics. One of his lectures was delivered in Manchester Cathedral; another in Gloucester Cathedral; and a third, to the Industrial Christian Fellowship. But the subjects Frank Field addresses must be faced by all of us who would 'love our neighbours as ourselves' – such subjects as 'The enduring value of work' and 'Monitoring the poor's welfare'.

I can't pretend that the book is always an easy read. Welfare Reform today is undoubtedly a very complex subject – but, as undoubtedly, it affects the lives of millions. It's a relief, however, that the book is spiced with a little humour. I loved the story of Sir Keith Joseph and the journalist Matthew Parris: meeting – some years ago – in a lift, at the Conservative Party Conference. They engaged in conversation, and, as the lift approached its destination, Sir Keith courteously expressed the hope that he would one day enjoy another journey in Matthew's lift. It was clear that Sir Keith thought

Matthew was the lift-man, when he was then but a keen party activist.

Perhaps, at the end of these three political party conferences, we might remind ourselves that all politicians are human; all get things wrong as well as right; but that they all have a high calling: to shape a just and caring society.

C. F. Andrews, the Christian priest, and close friend of Gandhi, who addressed himself to the social problems of India, defined love as 'the careful enquiry into the needs of others that enables one to give the exact help needed'.

Politicians may prefer to avoid the use of that word 'love'. But that is their calling: to wrestle with the details of that 'exact help', in a way which challenges and involves us all, whatever our party – or, indeed, our religion.

———— • ◆ • ————

65

Prayers for people in prison

Saturday 6 February 1999

When I was training for ordination, I was taught to remind myself each Saturday morning that it was the day between Good Friday and Easter Sunday, when Jesus was in the grave; and to pray, therefore, on Saturdays, for two very different sorts of people: those who'd just died, and those who were locked up in prison.

A friend of mine, confined to her home with an incurable disease, used to help me with my prayers for those in prison. Unable to get out, she felt it her vocation to pray for individual prisoners who could never be released – some of them on death row; and she'd ask me to pray for them. Since then, having to visit particular people in prison, or being asked to preach in prison chapels, I've never lacked contact with prisons and prisoners. One of the undergraduates to whom I was Chaplain in Cambridge, in the 1950s, has been in prison for years, and has been transferred to different prisons. I've visited him in jails in Durham, Wakefield, Nottingham; and the list goes on.

Recently, I've been helped in my prayers more than I can say by a book simply called *Prayers for People in Prison*. It's by a prison chaplain, William Noblett. To many people, life in prison is, understandably, almost another world: so Noblett's book is particularly valuable. It introduces you to different people, different jobs, different situations in prison – all of them real. But it also provides facts and figures where and when they're necessary, and reflects on some major subjects – like Evil itself.

You find yourself thinking about those who've just arrived in prison and those who've been there for years. You're confronted by the violence of prison life, and the pain, and the changes that take place in people, for good and ill; the light behind bars as well as the darkness.

Hardly a week goes by without our papers describing people like, for instance, the woman sentenced this week at Chester Crown Court to life in prison for stabbing to death her lover's wife. We may not feel like praying for her, or for people like her; but William Noblett provides words that may move our hearts to prayer:

> Father,
> In the depths of anguish
> you are there.
> In the brokenness of our lives
> you are there.
> In the torment we inflict on
> each other, you are there.
> No situation is beyond your presence.
> In our gestures, in our words,
> may we recognize you
> And in simple action – find you.

———◆·———

66

Valentines

Saturday 13 February 1999

There are rival claimants this year for the relics of St Valentine. They come from Glasgow, Dublin and Edgbaston – and his head, some say, was once buried in Winchester, though there's uncertainty as to where it lies now.

As an aged Anglican ecclesiastic, I don't find myself all that attracted to the subject of 'old bones', especially as some say that there were two St Valentines – one a bishop, and the other a priest – and that much of what is said about both of them is legend. I get much more worked up about the commercialization of St Valentine's Day. This year, the shops and the advertisement columns have been crowded with ludicrously expensive valentines of one sort and another, which, I think, debase the whole idea. But I tell myself to calm down on that as well. In advancing years you must be selective about the subjects on which you spend your energy!

But please don't think I'm against valentines: I'm for them, and would urge both young and old to indulge in them. But romance is best conveyed, I reckon, by simplicity: a simple poem, even a letter. And let no one with love in their heart think there's nothing of the poet in them. One of my favourite poems – 'First Meeting', by the fairly unknown poet A. S. J. Tessimond – begins just like a valentine:

> When I first met you I knew I had come at last home,
> Home after wandering . . . Long being lost;

And he goes on:

> . . . I was walking and talking and laughing
> Easily at last . . .
> And these words are the beginning of my thanks.

St Valentine himself – since we know so little about him – doesn't provide much raw material for our valentines; but there's help, I think, in, for instance, St Aelred, the abbot of that lovely abbey,

Rievaulx, in Yorkshire. He said: 'Friendship lies close to perfection'; and: 'to live without friends is to live like a beast'. And he added: 'Friendship is like a step to raise us to the love and knowledge of God.'

On the eve of St Valentine, I find myself thankful that my closest friends have done just that for me: they've taught me that prayer can be a kind of valentine that we send to God himself – in return for the gift of his love.

67

The mystery of Time

Saturday 20 February 1999

Those who listen to this programme, and a few weeks ago voted Shakespeare the 'Personality of the Millennium', would not by then have seen the film *Shakespeare in Love*, which I saw a couple of nights ago. It's a marvellous film; and it's not surprising that it's drawing plaudits from everywhere, and filling the cinemas, though its story is almost entirely untrue. What I hope is that the film will draw even more than those who voted to treat Shakespeare as their guide in these months before the Millennium.

We can't be certain of Shakespeare's religion, but one thing is without doubt: few people have thought more on the mystery of Time. Most of us simply take Time for granted. Shakespeare has four or five dozen wise and beautiful sayings on Time. He speaks of 'the dial hand of time' – which moves so silently and stealthily. In *Macbeth*, Banquo says to the witches: 'If you can look into the seeds of time, and say which grain will grow and which will not . . .' But, of course, none of us can do that.

'Time has a wallet,' writes Shakespeare. What an image that is! We can store valuable memories in Time's wallet, like gold pieces – though alas, not all our memories are gold. The Green Movement, I think, should publish a pamphlet this year on what Shakespeare called 'sluttish' Time. Sometimes he could not be more simple.

'Make use of time' he says. At other times, he captures the mysteriousness of Time. He speaks of 'the dark backward and abysm of Time': that you can look back only so far in Time, and then things get lost in the dark of Time past. He speaks of 'Time's best jewel' hid in 'Time's chest'. Each of us, I imagine, could say what is the 'best jewel' Time has given us.

Scientists, historians, musicians, all of us, have something to say about Time. But it remains a mystery. It would be marvellous if the Millennium made us all confront that mystery. I rather hope that the Dome – somehow – will enable all those who enter it to do just that.

Shakespeare encourages us to 'take upon's the Mystery of things as if we were God's spies.' This year, as we approach the Millennium, I think we're all challenged to take upon's the Mystery of Time.

<hr />

68

VJ Day

Monday 21 June 1999

I find myself surprised, after the VE celebrations, that there seem to be so few plans to commemorate the fiftieth anniversary of VJ Day, in a few weeks' time. My *Thought for the Day* is really a story in preparation for that event.

One evening, nearly 40 years ago, when I was Chaplain of Trinity College, Cambridge, I was sitting at dinner, next to the then Professor of Physics, Otto Frisch. We talked first about his childhood in Austria, and then about his doing research in Hamburg in the early 1930s. He said he tried at first to pretend that Hitler was best ignored; but when Jews – like himself – began to be beaten up, he realized he must leave Germany. He came to England, after a time in Copenhagen. But it was in 1943 that he was one of a dozen scientists who were shipped across the Atlantic in order to be part of the team working on the atomic bomb at Los Alamos, in the deserts of New Mexico.

Frisch said that when they exploded the first atomic bomb, it looked like 'a red-hot elephant standing balanced on its trunk'. He recounted how, after the explosion of the bomb, there were lively discussions as to how it should be used. Should it be used at all? Should a demonstration be staged on some uninhabited island, with the enemy invited to watch it? Some people were saying that scientists should stick to matters of their own competence. Others thought that an ostrich-like attitude.

They didn't know, Frisch said, where or when the bomb they had made would be dropped. Then, one day, three weeks after the first bomb had been exploded, there was a sudden noise of running footsteps and yelling voices, and someone opened the door of Frisch's laboratory, and shouted, 'Hiroshima has been destroyed! About 100,000 people have been killed.' Frisch said he felt first uneasy, and then sick, as he saw how many of his friends were rushing to the telephones to book tables in the restaurant of a local hotel to celebrate. And, only a few days later, a second bomb was dropped on Nagasaki; and few of those at Los Alamos could see any moral reason for that. Frisch said he thought that the new and terrifying and god-like power had gone to the heads of those with the power of decision.

Well, whether those decisions were right or wrong, they were clearly momentous, for the Japanese war came quickly to an end.

And surely we ought to be preparing to commemorate all those events appropriately – not least by praying: 'Our father . . . deliver us from evil, and help us to see what actions we should be taking now to go with our prayer.'

69

My unconquerable soul

Monday 23 August 1999

It's 150 years today since the poet W. E. Henley was born. Very few read his poems now; but lots of people quote his phrases, probably without knowing who wrote them: 'Bloody, but unbowed'; 'I am the master of my fate: I am the Captain of my soul'.

William Ernest Henley was born in Gloucester, the son of a book-seller. From boyhood, he suffered from tubercular arthritis, and had one foot amputated. To save the other, in his twenties he went to Edinburgh and spent a year there in the infirmary in the care of a great surgeon, Joseph Lister.

It was while he was in hospital that he was introduced to Robert Louis Stevenson, who became a close friend, and they wrote plays together. Stevenson acknowledged Henley as the inspiration behind Long John Silver in *Treasure Island*.

It was in 1875, when he was in Edinburgh, that Henley had a sequence of poems published called *Hospital Sketches*. They're a striking record of his grim ordeal. The best known poem – the defiant and stoic 'Invictus' – came from that series of poems. I've sometimes heard people speak slightingly of Henley's verses, and specially of that one:

> Out of the night that covers me,
>   Black as the Pit from pole to pole,
> I thank whatever gods may be
>   For my unconquerable soul.

As someone who, in the course of his ministry, has quite often to visit people for whom the future is bleak and the present full of pain, I rarely myself feel able to speak with anything but respect, admiration and thankfulness whenever I encounter courage. I think now of Martin, whom I used to visit when he was in an iron lung for years, but was always an inspiration to visit.

We all need courage sometimes – even if it's only our very last hours that demand that courage from us – as they did from many of the victims of the earthquake in Turkey. But now, of course, it's the courage to go on going on that those who've survived will require as they face such a barren future.

'Be of good courage' is a phrase that comes often in the Bible. It's a spiritual quality which reveals the spiritual nature that lies at the very heart of us all. Thank God for those who display it.

May we have the courage of an 'unconquerable soul' when we need it. And may we cherish and revere it in others.

70

Divinity through humanity

Monday 30 August 1999

Last week, I went to see the new statue of Christ, by Mark Wallinger, that now stands opposite the National Gallery, on a plinth in Trafalgar Square that has been vacant for a century and a half. I went to see it with a friend, who immediately said: 'It's too human, isn't it?' I didn't want simply to disagree – he was making an important point But his comment made me recall an incident which has been in and out of my mind ever since Cardinal Hume died.

A few years ago, the Cardinal came to preach at Gray's Inn. He preached a memorable sermon; but what was even more memorable for me was what happened immediately after the service, in the robing room.

'Eric,' asked the Cardinal 'do you sweat when you preach?' I was so surprised by the question that I could only manage a nearly meaningless reply. 'I sweat profusely,' said the Cardinal. 'My shirt is wringing wet. Where can I change it before lunch?' I pointed to the door of the loo; but at that moment, half a dozen of what are called Benchers of the Inn were making for it. 'Can't I change it here?' pressed the Cardinal. 'Er . . . yes' I said, somewhat hesitantly. And he began to strip off his shirt.

As he was standing there, naked above the waist, with his braces dangling, a very aged and infirm Bencher slowly entered the room, and, unable to believe his eyes – that this was the man he'd seen in Chapel, only minutes before, clad in scarlet and fine linen – simply stood and gaped.

'Yes,' said the Cardinal, turning to him with a winning smile: 'I *am* a man!'

Godliness – indeed, divinity – can best be revealed in this world, Jesus taught us, through our humanity.

Of course, the idea that God – or 'the gods' – have made themselves present in this world in human form is widespread in the history of religions. But the Christian religion is unique in the way it speaks of God making himself known in a life of self-sacrificial love, and of God, in a human life, taking suffering and evil onto himself, with the climax of that life in the Crucifixion.

It's the echo of that in the humanity of the statue in Trafalgar Square that I think makes it such a marvellous work. It's true: it's an ordinary, ordinary young man. But it challenges those of us who look at it to reveal our divinity through our humanity.

71

Dependence, independence, interdependence

Monday 6 September 1999

It's striking how many areas of the world just now are painfully having to grapple with the problems of independence and interdependence: East Timor, Northern Ireland, Israel and Palestine, and so on. But I think it would be wrong to put any of those problem areas wholly in a package marked 'Foreign Affairs'.

I so well remember when I was a student in my twenties, with my own clutch of personal problems, how the then Dean of my College,

Eric Abbott, a brilliant counsellor and friend, said to me, caringly, one day: 'You need to work at three words: Dependence, independence and interdependence.'

It was so easy to be over-dependent on one person. It was as easy to adopt a kind of bogus independence of everyone. The problem was to discover a true and proper interdependence. I had to work at all that for twenty years or more – some of them quite painful. And I never feel I've entirely finished with the subject.

Eric Abbott became Dean of Westminster in 1959, and died in 1983. To the end, he remained a close friend and counsellor to me, as he did to many.

One day in 1963, I happened to be passing Westminster Abbey, when, clearly, there was something of importance going on. Official cars were arriving and departing. Flags were flying. There was a crowd of people at the entrance, mostly black, many of them in national costume. I soon discovered it was a service to celebrate the independence of Nigeria. 'Who's preaching?' I asked a friendly verger. 'The Dean,' he said. 'Any chance of a seat?' I asked. 'Of course,' he said, and led me to one in the nave.

I wondered what Eric, Dean of Westminster, would make of such a prestigious occasion. I need not have wondered. As everyone left the Abbey – cabinet ministers, diplomats, Nigerian leaders – you could hear them saying what a marvellous service (and sermon) it had been.

But what was the subject of the sermon? It was those three words – dependence, independence and interdependence – which, said the preacher, both individuals and nations have to work at. It was a sermon which was profoundly Christian, yet would speak as profoundly to a Nigerian Muslim. The Dean said that he had in mind 'that inarticulate prayer which every human heart is making'.

This morning, as we hold in our thoughts the peoples and pains of such different parts of the world, those three words may have something to say to each one of us:

Dependence,
Independence,
Interdependence.

———— • ◆ • ————

72

A Passage to India

Monday 13 September 1999

It's a curious coincidence that this weekend, as we've been watching the changing situation between Indonesia and East Timor, in India, elections have been going on. There the democratic process has been working. Musing on this fact, I took down from my shelves that wonderful novel about India, so sensitively filmed – E. M. Forster's *A Passage to India*.

Forty years ago, when I was a Chaplain in Cambridge, I used sometimes to conduct Evensong in that glorious Chapel of King's College, and Forster, although an avowed agnostic, would often attend. He was not far off 80 then, and would potter in and out of the Chapel – for purely aesthetic reasons, he would aver. It was difficult to believe that this little old man was the author of such a great novel about such a great country. He had written it out of love for India and its people.

In 1906, Forster had become tutor to a rich young Indian Muslim, Syed Ross Masood, who was waiting to go up to Oxford. That friendship altered Forster's life. So when he first visited India, six years later, he had already had a closer relationship with India than many of the ruling British in India were ever likely to achieve – if, indeed, they thought that relationship desirable.

When he visited India again, in 1921, it was a time of high political drama. Mahatma Gandhi had emerged as a leader. And when *A Passage to India* was published, in 1924, the rights and wrongs of the British Raj were much in the news. *A Passage to India* is about many things – not least, friendship between different members of different races. It's about good government, and bringing order out of chaos – or, at least, out of muddle and squalor – so that education and medicine can be given a chance. It's about justice, and about God in different religions from one's own. 'God is here,' says Mrs Moore, when she wanders into a mosque.

In the final court scene in Forster's novel, he paints a marvellous portrait of the punkah-wallah who pulls the rope that works the fan that cools the court, as if to say, the punkah-wallah is as important as the magistrate. The magistrate insists that some people – English ladies and gentlemen – literally climb down off the platform in the court. 'A platform,' he says, 'confers authority.'

A Passage to India is, not least, about authority.

This morning, let us all in heart and mind take a passage to India, and to East Timor; and let us think thankfully of what we have received in our country that we have yet to share with the people of other parts of our one world.

———— • ◆ • ————

73

No future without forgiveness

Saturday 8 January 2000

It's always dangerous to say what you think was the best Christmas present you received; but, certainly, I didn't receive a better present this year than Desmond Tutu's book, *No Future Without Forgiveness*, which I've just finished. It's his personal account of the deliberations of South Africa's Truth and Reconciliation Commission, of which he was Chairman.

Of course, you can think of what he has to say as though it simply concerned South Africa, and the history of how that country dealt with a particular situation: when apartheid came to an end. That's important enough, God knows. But the real importance of Desmond Tutu's testimony, I believe, is that he describes an astonishing experience in the way human beings like ourselves can deal with the problem of reconciliation – in South Africa's case, after terrible atrocities.

It's almost unbearable to be taken through some of the confessions of ghastly inhumanity and brutality – killings, mutilations – that are confessed by both sides. Even while Nelson Mandela was in prison, plans were laid for his murder. But it was he who initiated this process of reconciliation.

Desmond Tutu sums up what he has to say in a story: of three United States ex-servicemen standing in front of the Viet Nam

Memorial in Washington. One asks: 'Have you forgiven those who held you prisoner?' 'I will never forgive them,' replies the man he addresses. His mate says: 'Then it seems they still have you in prison, don't they?'

That's what Desmond Tutu is trying to drive home.

What he has to say is, of course, about justice; but, if one dare say so, it sets its sights even higher than justice – on healing.

One of my jobs for nearly twenty years was to be Chaplain to the judges and barristers of Gray's Inn. I would like every judge, and magistrate, and probation officer, in Britain today, to have to confront what Desmond Tutu has to say: that reconciliation means more than a narrow definition of justice. And that concerns not only people in the law: it's for all and any of us involved in situations where reconciliation is desperately needed: in, for instance, marriage and family breakdowns.

It's as relevant to Northern Ireland and Kosovo as it is to South Africa. It relates to people who may fetch up in Britain with a criminal record, and how we deal with them.

No Future Without Forgiveness. Those four words enshrine a truth that all of us need to learn in our deep heart's core this eighth day of a New Year and New Era.

Desmond Tutu, I believe, has something to say to us all about a new beginning.

———— •◆• ————

74

To the altar of God

Saturday 15 January 2000

Last night they were celebrating in Rome the centenary of the first performance of Puccini's opera *Tosca*. Last week, I went to a superb concert performance of it here in London.

Tosca is an extraordinary opera. It starts in a church in Rome; but, by the end, we've encountered revolution, police corruption, torture, murder, jealousy, attempted rape, and finally suicide.

The remarkable thing about opera is that although often the events that take place before our eyes are tragic and terrible – as, of course, are the events in many of Shakespeare's plays – we go home saying 'It was a marvellous evening.'

With an opera, the singing and the music may, indeed, have been wonderful; and what is portrayed before our eyes may have had huge dramatic power. In *Tosca* you are drawn alongside two innocent people trapped in the whirlpool of politics, and you see them sacrifice themselves on the altar of loyalty and love. There's no doubt in my mind that Puccini, in *Tosca*, wanted to evoke the whole gamut of human emotions: from the innocence of a shepherd boy, whose singing introduces the final act, to the very darkest evil.

It's no accident that the opera begins before an altar. The hero, Cavaradossi, is an artist, at work on a painting of Mary Magdalene to go above the altar. Puccini himself had been a church organist. The church choir, the church bells, the altar, are never far away in *Tosca*. But if Puccini knew a lot about the church, you feel he also knew a lot about the world, and about the reality of human nature.

When I was sitting listening to the centenary concert, a memory flashed through my mind of my theological college days, over 50 years ago, and our Principal, Eric Abbott, saying to us one day: 'When you leave the altar, always envisage when you will go to it again – and say to yourself the verse of the Psalm: "I will go unto the altar of God"; and say that verse again and again during the day, whatever you're doing and wherever you are. And take with you to the altar all that you are and all that you've done and been – for good and ill. Even in your last hour you will be able to say: "I will go unto the altar of God".'

Tosca is an opera that evokes in us a sense of life in the shadow of the altar of God; but it leaves us wistful for life with that altar at its centre. And the challenge is not just to Cavaradossi but to us all; to bring our politics, and sex, our tragedies and all that gives us joy, to the altar of God.

———————— •◆• ————————

75

Moral anger

Saturday 22 January 2000

Round the corner from where I live, in Kennington, South London, is the Imperial War Museum. I suspect it's the most misunderstood museum there is: for many people still imagine it's there primarily to glorify war. In fact, its job is to tell the story of war 'as it is': that's to say, the two world wars and other military operations in which Britain has been involved since 1914.

In the past weeks, the Museum has been holding an exhibition of the paintings of Christopher Nevinson, an artist who did his best work in the First World War. A limp prevented him enlisting as a soldier, so he volunteered as an ambulance driver in the Red Cross. Within a few weeks he'd been shipped to France, and found himself looking after the wounded, dead and dying, in a covered goods yard outside Dunkirk.

Nevinson's paintings of that ghastly scene were an antidote to the official propagandist depiction of the war and, indeed, to the jingoism of journalists. He managed to communicate, through his paintings – much as Wilfred Owen did through his poems – the horror and pity of war.

I'm sorry to say that clergy were among the voluble opposition to Nevinson's paintings when they were first exhibited in London. He said he was proud to think that three canons had preached against 'me and my pictures'. General Sir Ian Hamilton said that the appeal of Nevinson's works lay in their quality of truth. 'On canvas,' he said, 'what Nevinson painted became a symbol of world tragedy.'

There was, and is, a protesting vigour about Nevinson's art: a questioning moral anger. None other than John Buchan did what he could to see that the paintings were not censored – which was the aim and object of some of those in power.

As I stood this week before those paintings, I found myself thankful for our human capacity for 'moral anger' – that has shone out from the prophets of old and even before them, for our gifts of pity and compassion, and for the skill and sympathy of artists such as Nevinson.

But I found myself also asking where that 'moral anger' is now best shown – in peace time, so called – in a world governed by a free market and global economics, which do so little to diminish the huge disparity between the rich and the starving poor.

Christopher Nevinson claimed to have no religion; but I found myself thankful to God for him: for reminding us that 'moral anger' is one of God's best gifts to human beings.

'Touch me with noble anger' prayed Shakespeare's King Lear.

76

Sport

Saturday 29 January 2000

The subject of sport raises huge questions – not least, the Tyson fight tonight.

Saturday, as long as I can remember, has been sport day. And I'm going back 60 years, to when my childhood hero, Alex James, played for Arsenal, and Kenneth Farnes – killed, alas, in the war – played cricket for my home county, Essex, and England.

But nothing makes me feel my age more than when I hear myself saying that money has largely destroyed sport as I knew it; and local football has been dwarfed by the major clubs – sponsored by big money, advertising and TV, with English teams no longer English; and with huge market pressures to buy the kit and clobber associated with the major clubs; and with so much sport now being spectator, not participant.

As I say, I feel my age when such thoughts possess me, until I meet and share them – as I did last week – with Edward, who's 10, and his brother Dennis, who's 12. These are ordinary youngsters, living on a London housing estate; and they agreed with me, and said they can't afford to go to see their favourite team play – which happens to be Spurs. Add to that the sale of so many local sports facilities as sites for supermarkets, and the pressure on schools to concentrate on anything but sport – and I believe you have a serious situation.

But what I've said so far has to be set alongside the huge decline, almost demotion, of youth work, certainly in London. And sport and youth work used to do something of great value. It built up your ability to work in teams, and to discover and develop God-given gifts, not least in the not-so-academic.

I have little doubt that we urgently need a commission on the future of youth work including sport – on how we can rediscover the amateur ideal. I remember the dynamic effect of the Albemarle Report on the Youth Service in 1958.

I take sport as my subject today not least because, as a parish priest in South London, I learnt once and for all the human importance of youth work, to which the churches made a major contribution. And much of my experience in later years has persuaded me that, far from that work being outdated or irrelevant, in hugely changed circumstances, and in a society with – for better and worse – very different values, not least in sport, the need for it now is as great as ever.

77

O you wonder!

Saturday 20 May 2000

Whenever I'm privileged to take a newborn baby in my arms, two phrases of Shakespeare come often into my mind: 'Thy life's a miracle' and 'O you wonder!'

In my nearly 50 years now as a priest, I also often think of that Noel Coward song: 'Other people's babies – that's my life'; for, year after year, I've been privileged to share the joy of parents at the birth of their children. And you soon learn that when a baby is born, the parents most often want to say a heartfelt 'Thank you' to someone.

And most religions provide for a kind of language for saying that 'Thank you'.

I've no doubt that Tony and Cherie Blair have hearts full of thankfulness today – not least because birth is still such a precarious business, and because you're so dependent on the skill and care of others.

It's sometimes said, somewhat cynically, that a priest's ministry is concerned primarily with 'hatches, matches and despatches'. Well. I would have to say that the part of ministry that has to do with 'hatches' has taught me a very great deal.

First of all: the naming of a child says something to us all of the mystery of our unique identity – the uniqueness of every one of us.

When I was a parish priest in inner South London, we had a huge hostel for the homeless on the borders of the parish. And I soon learnt that I had to do more than proclaim the spiritual value of each child, important as that was. But it would have been a blasphemy to proclaim, in the name of God, 'This child is a child of God' and do nothing about its housing, its health care, and its education, and to see that the parents had an income – which probably, of course, meant a job.

Curiously, the first child I christened in South London was a Nigerian, the child of a medical student. I christened him Olayemi Olusola Odanye – I had to learn the names in order to pronounce them, and they've stuck in my mind for 40 years! I learnt that we all belong to one another, need one another, and that a Nigerian child is as valued and valuable as a British child.

So, today, as we rejoice with Tony and Cherie Blair; I cannot myself see this event only as a private and family event. It is that, of course. But much of the work of a prime minister – whatever his party and politics – in the end centres, surely, on the welfare of vulnerable children like the Blair's new-born son.

So I say again: 'O you wonder!' 'Thy life's a miracle!'

78

What if?

Saturday 27 May 2000

The title of a book sometimes stirs the imagination as much as the book itself. Earlier this week, in a bookshop, I saw a book with the title: *What If? Military Historians Imagine What Might Have Been*. It was, of course, a title calculated to stir the mind and heart of those who can still remember Dunkirk, as many of us will this weekend.

I didn't buy the book; but when I got the bus home, my mind couldn't stop racing with that question, 'What if?' – not only 'What if Dunkirk hadn't gone the way it did?', but 'What if Shakespeare had never been born?' We know that plague hit Stratford-upon-Avon the very year he was born, and wiped out a lot of the population. It could so easily have wiped *him* out.

'What if Bach' – the 250th anniversary of whose death we're celebrating this year – 'What if Bach had never been born?'

'What if Jesus had never been born?' – 'What if Mary's pregnancy had come to an early end?' As a priest I've spent a good deal of time with families who were bereaved of the baby they'd been expecting.

'What if Judas had never been born?'

As soon as I got home, the day I picked up that book, I happened to catch sight, on my shelves, of the book my mother had given me for my twenty-first birthday, in 1946. 'What if my mother had never been born?' I thought. She was one of ten in a Victorian family in Camden Town. No mother – no me.

Of course, there's something more than a little scary about that question. But there's also something which makes you revalue people and events and life that you'd perhaps begun to take for granted.

'What if?' can be a form of prayer – and thanksgiving.

'What if I'd never met my friend Robert? – or Gwen?'

> 'Some enchanted evening,
> You may see a stranger,
> Across a crowded room'

– and from that moment, life is different.

But 'What if you missed seeing that stranger?' Life would have been different again because of that.

Part of prayer is simply wondering – in the presence of God. Everyone, I think, has the capacity for wonder – that's one reason why I believe everyone's religious.

Prayer is a kind of observing what's there, and consuming and savouring it, or what's not there, and reflecting on the mystery of its absence.

'What if?' is a question that can help us discover – or rediscover – the wondering part of us.

———— •◆• ————

79

Religious education

Saturday 3 June 2000

A young priest friend of mine, who lives in the heart of the East End of London, decided recently not to give up his priesthood, but to take on teaching, full-time, in the local Church of England school. He's living in a predominantly Muslim area; and, in fact 95 per cent of the students in his school are Muslims. There are now very few Church of England families in the area, far too few to warrant a separate Church of England school.

I hasten to add that the purpose of the school is, of course, to educate its students for life; and I underline that it's not its purpose to change anyone from Islam to anything else. The teaching of the school is, of course, carefully thought out, so that the students learn about many world religions, as well as Christianity and Islam. They probably end up with an increased ability to understand their own religion, and also to compare and contrast it with the religions of other people.

Quite often, the students find they have more in common with others than they had imagined – reverence for God, and a deeper understanding of what's right and what's wrong. But they're not simply learning about morals: they're learning who they are, and about meaning and purpose in the world of today.

It's worth saying that Britain is probably unique in having Religious Education as a compulsory requirement in all schools, not just in church and religious schools. It may be that it's teaching like that in the school I've described, which is resulting in a huge increase in the number of people in our universities who are now studying theology – people of different races and religions. They're not studying that subject as they probably would have done in earlier generations, with a view to, say, getting ordained in the priesthood of their religion. They are interested in pursuing the truth of what lies at the heart of religion; indeed, at the heart of life. And that, surely, is something that can only be good.

I speak on this particular subject, on this particular morning, because the thoughts of many Christians will be turning towards the celebration of Pentecost – Whitsuntide – next weekend when the Christian New Testament tells of people coming together from different races; and instead of there being Babel, a meaningless babble, they understood one another, through the gift of the Holy Spirit.

Whatever leads us to a more profound understanding of each other – across the barriers of race and religion – must surely be 'of God'.

———— •◆• ————

80

Bridges

Saturday 10 June 2000

There's something about a bridge which fascinates us all: Tower Bridge, the Forth Bridge, Sydney Harbour Bridge. And most of us can remember some bridge we stood on as a child and watched water flowing beneath us.

Bridges have played their part in history: 'How Horatio Kept the Bridge'. In the Second World War: 'A Bridge Too Far' at Arnhem.

There are great bridges of fiction – like Thornton Wilder's

The Bridge of San Luis Rey, which records the stories of those who were killed when the bridge collapsed, and the stories of those who, by the luck of the draw – or the hand of Providence – escaped.

Bridges are often associated with tragedy. They always remain places of danger. So we say, with worldly wisdom: 'Never cross a bridge until you come to it.'

Bridges that span a river seem to speak of and symbolize separate worlds that have been joined.

As a priest, I can never entirely forget that one of the Latin words for priest – *pontifex* – has the Latin word for bridge at the heart of it: challenging priests always to be bridge-builders where there are broken lives and broken families, and gulfs between classes and races. But there's a priest in everyone. To be human is to be a priest. In the end – or rather, in the beginning – everyone's a priest. And we all have to learn about 'The Bridge Over Troubled Waters'.

The opening of the Millennium Bridge over the Thames has had a peculiar fascination for me. From the age of 14 to 21, I worked at a riverside wharf on the South Bank of the Thames, just a hundred or so yards from where the Millennium Bridge now begins. Each day, and many times a day, I looked across the Thames to that unparalleled view of St Paul's crowned by its dome, with often its cross of gold shining in the sun.

I'm looking forward to walking across the new bridge some time this weekend. It's fully open for the first time today. As I walk, I shall think thankfully of those I worked with during what now seems an age ago – and gratefully of those who have designed, constructed and lit the new Millennium Bridge. And I think I shall sing to myself:

> There's one more river
> And that's the river of Jordan . . .
> There's one more river to cross.

And Love can build a bridge.

———————

81

The mystery and miracle of existence

Saturday 12 August 2000

It often happens, I find, that when the newspapers are full of some major subject, something happens in your life that gives you a particular insight on the subject. That was so for me recently, when the subject of the cloning of human embryos was hitting the headlines.

My phone rang. It was a couple I'd married only last year. The baby they were now expecting was brain-damaged by an infection. At that stage, no one quite knew how serious the damage was. We met and talked over the kind of complex decisions that might be involved. A few days later, they phoned again. This time, the news was as bad as it could be. The baby – Alexander, they'd called him – had been born, but was dead, after only five months in the womb.

I went to the hospital as soon as I could. The obstetrician couldn't have been more helpful. She'd said: 'Had Alexander lived he would have had no power even to turn himself over in bed.' So, mercifully, the decision to deliver him was not a borderline case.

Sitting with his parents in the ward, cradling the lifeless Alexander on my lap, my thoughts and emotions were many and powerful. Sympathy, of course, for the grieving parents; and admiration for the skill and wisdom of the obstetric surgeon and the nurses.

The hospital was one noted for its research. Perhaps at some future date it might save the life of babies like Alexander. But, now, his lifeless body confronted us with the difference between life and death – and with the precariousness and danger of every birth; with the mystery of fertilization, followed by the processes of growth in the womb that result, in most instances, not simply in the birth of a body – with all its complex and wonderful structures – but in the birth of a unique person.

The pink, lifeless form on my lap, that might have been a child with a life ahead of him, in some odd way renewed in me the mystery and miracle of existence as well as the tragedy of death.

Next week, it's anticipated that the government's long-awaited report on the cloning of human embryos will be published.

I am thankful to have been reminded at this particular time of the unremitting struggle in hospitals to save life; that the ethical problems involved are not simply abstract, but have human beings like Alexander and his parents at the heart of them. Indeed, at the heart of them are unique, wonderful and sacred beings like ourselves.

———— ◆ ————

82

Creative suffering

Saturday 26 August 2000

'A Tale of Two Women' is what I might call my *Thought for Today*.

The first, Constance Babington-Smith, died recently, aged 87. She was remarkable, not least for her war-time work of interpreting air reconnaissance photographs, enabling the location of sites in Germany, where V1 and V2 bombs were being tested, to be identified. Her first book was called *Evidence in Camera*. She wrote another, after the war, of a very different kind. She'd become a convert to the Orthodox Church, and wrote the life of the second woman I have in mind: Julia de Beausobre, who'd already written her own account of her life, calling it *The Woman Who Could Not Die*.

Few books have helped me more.

Julia de Beausobre's first husband had been killed in the Lubyanka Russian prison camp. She herself was often at death's door in that camp. When I first met her – nearly 50 years ago – I'd read of her ordeal, and had expected to meet someone broken and emaciated. But I was astonished at her radiance.

I was interviewing her at a lunch-hour group of civil servants in the parish in Westminster where I was a curate. I asked her how she had coped with all that she'd suffered. Her answer was unforgettable: 'It was simple really,' she said. 'If, in response to the evil that was done to me and people like me, I'd sought revenge, that would have done the work of those who were imprisoning me. And they would have succeeded in getting me to add to the evil in the world. My task was to diminish the evil. And there was only one way to do that: the way of prayer, praying for those who were being cruel to me and others in that camp.'

It was obvious to me that that 'the way of prayer' had transformed Julia. She'd given a talk in 1940 which she'd called 'Creative Suffering'. It's been reprinted many times. Julia had come to believe that 'Hell is the very place in which to seek and find God.' And few people knew more about hell-on-earth than she did.

Later in life, she married Sir Lewis Namier, the British historian, himself of Russian origin.

She died in 1977.

Constance Babington-Smith's life of Julia was called *A Russian Christian in the West*.

At the end of this fortnight of such terrible travail for the people of Russia, it seems appropriate to remember those two remarkable women who desired the best for the Russian people, but whose desire for us all was that we should learn more of the way of 'creative suffering'.

———— ◆ ————

83

Unless I be relieved by prayer

Saturday 2 September 2000

Shakespeare's *The Tempest*, with Vanessa Redgrave as Prospero, has been playing to full houses at the Globe Theatre on the South Bank of the Thames, for the last five months. When I went to a performance recently, I was conscious of a curious mix of emotions – not least because it was on that very site that, 60 years ago, I used to sit in my office each morning, dealing with orders for deliveries to and from Thames barges, and to horses and carts and vans, in those wartime days.

Bankside was then a very different place. Now, with its Globe

Theatre, it's in some ways back to what it was in Shakespeare's time. But there were other reasons for my confused emotions. Several close friends of mine have departed this life recently, and I suspect it was the bereaved 'me' who heard afresh those powerful 'last lines' of *The Tempest*, which Prospero speaks:

> And my ending is despair
> Unless I be relieved by prayer.

Were those last words simply what Shakespeare put into the mouth of Prospero, I wondered, or would he have meant them himself? We're fairly certain that in 1607 Shakespeare paid for his 27-year-old brother Edmund's funeral, a few hundred yards along the river from the Globe, at what is now Southwark Cathedral, and paid for the great bell to be tolled.

Would he have despaired at his young actor brother's death, had he not been 'relieved by prayer'? I'd be surprised if Shakespeare hadn't meant exactly what he said. I've spent nearly 50 years now conducting funerals; and I've known very few brothers or sisters – or fathers or mothers, or sons or daughters – who haven't wanted to be 'relieved by prayer' when their loved ones have died.

Shakespeare seems to encourage us to despise Macbeth's cynicism when he says, 'There's nothing serious in mortality.'

Nowadays, maybe we fall to prayer when death comes to those we love, but fail to explore the unseen world until those final moments catch up with us, or we with them.

This weekend, I'm very conscious, as many will be, that it's the anniversary of the outbreak of the Second World War. I'm well aware of several of the friends of my youth who lost their lives in that war, not least in the Battle of Britain. Their friends and relatives will be asking still the simple question, 'Where are they now?' And many of us would have to say, with Shakespeare:

> My ending is despair
> Unless I be relieved by prayer.

———— •◆• ————

84

The flame of the Everlasting Love

Saturday 9 September 2000

The Last Night of the Proms tonight brings to an end a memorable season that has commemorated in eighteen of the Proms the 250th anniversary of the death of Johann Sebastian Bach, including an outstanding performance of his *Mass in B Minor*.

The most memorable Prom for me, however, was the centenary performance of Elgar's masterpiece, *The Dream of Gerontius*, which kept on reminding me of the first performance of *Gerontius* I ever heard, on 10 May 1941. It was at the Queen's Hall, where the Proms began – then close by Broadcasting House. I was just 16 years old; but that performance of *Gerontius*, conducted by Dr Malcolm Sargent, did much to give me a sense that life is a journey – a pilgrimage – from this life to the next

In 1941, that was a message I needed to hear; for the very evening of that concert, as soon as I'd reached home, ten miles East of London, the siren sounded; and for five moonlit hours German bombers dropped a huge number of incendiaries and high explosives on London. Fifteen hundred people were killed that night, and many more injured, and the House of Commons, several City churches, and the Queen's Hall itself – which, as I've said, I'd been in that afternoon, were all destroyed. Only this year, a plaque has been placed in Upper Regent Street to commemorate Queen's Hall, and its destruction that night.

What I can never forget is that, within the space of so few hours, I myself experienced transcendent glory in and through music and the indescribable inhumanity of man to man. Something of those twin realities is, of course, part of the experience of us all.

Each year since 1941 I've tried to attend a performance of *Gerontius* as a kind of personal pilgrimage: to renew in me the sense of life itself as a pilgrimage. And always within me there has been the memory of that night in 1941, and its contrasting glory and misery. I've found inspiration not only in the music of *Gerontius* but in the words of Cardinal Newman, to which Elgar set his matchless music.

Gerontius doesn't evade the reality of our human capacity for both glory and misery; but there's a single sentence in the poem which I think lies at the very heart of it, and which is, so to speak, the 'pilgrim's way' from misery to glory. Newman writes: 'Learn that the flame of the Everlasting Love doth burn 'ere it transform.'

• ◆ •

85

The worst form of government

Saturday 16 September 2000

At this sixtieth anniversary of the Battle of Britain, many of us will be thankfully remembering Winston Churchill, who so eloquently voiced the nation's gratitude to those who fought in that battle. Churchill also said, seven years later, 'Democracy is the worst form of government except all those other forms that have been tried from time to time.' This last week, many of us have been forced to think again about 'Democracy in Britain'.

It means, of course, 'the rule of the people'; but it's not always easy to see what that implies. Certainly it means in Britain that our representatives are elected after prolonged public discussion concerning the candidates and the issues involved. Equally important is the voters' ability to turn their representatives out of office. And here in Britain we know that a General Election is now not far off.

In our democracy we believe in majority rule, but we also believe in the political rights of minorities. It's important in a programme of religious comment like *Thought for the Day* to underline that the will of the people is not necessarily God's will. Dictators, and people who lead uprisings, often claim to 'speak for the people' – and sometimes do. But theologians, like the American, Reinhold Niebuhr, have given special attention to the bearing of the Christian view of human nature on the question of democracy.

As a student, just after the war, I listened with rapt attention to Niebuhr lecturing, both in Westminster and Edinburgh, on 'The

Nature and Destiny of Man' and on 'Moral Man and Immoral Society'. I knew I was hearing not only a great theologian and philosopher but a prophet for our times and our post-war society. We were turning our backs then on dictators who had seized power and had misled whole nations.

The lip-service we pay to democracy tends to cloak some of its recurring problems. It can lead to rule on behalf of some group that dislikes its procedures and is impatient with its corporate decisions. There's a discipline to democracy and a price to be paid for it in peace time – which has to be paid by each one of us.

There are various ways of fighting for a democracy. Our Spitfire pilots did it, thank God, 60 years ago – with great bravery and self-sacrifice. Otherwise we wouldn't be here today. But you have to go on fighting to preserve democracy year after year. I think it means respecting the self-respect of others, and remembering that 'We're all "members one of another"' – to use St Paul's words; and that 'We're all one body' – the strong and the weak together.

86

If you dig deeper

Saturday 21 October 2000

Billy Elliot – the film about the boy ballet dancer from a Durham pit village – is all the rage at the moment.

I was delighted to discover that Lee Hall, who wrote the book of the film, also wrote a farce called *Wittgenstein on Tyne*, about the two wartime years the great philosopher spent as a hospital porter in Newcastle.

When I went to be Chaplain of Trinity College, Cambridge in 1955, memories of Wittgenstein were still green. He had died of cancer only four years before, but was still dominating the world of philosophy. He was born an Austrian Jew, in 1889, but had become a naturalized British subject in 1938. In the First World War he'd told one of his fellow prisoners that he'd most like to be a priest. The great Cambridge philosophers G. E. Moore and Bertrand Russell soon regarded the young Wittgenstein as a friend and colleague, rather than as a student.

I suppose his most famous saying was: 'Whereof one cannot speak, thereof one must be silent.' I wish, over the years, I'd treated those words with rather more respect.

Wittgenstein was a shy and reclusive character. He worked for a while as an elementary schoolmaster in a village school, and as an assistant in a monastery garden. For a time, he turned from philosophy to sculpture, and was only reluctantly persuaded by his English friends to return to philosophy. He became a Fellow of Trinity College, Cambridge, and a professor; but in the Second World War he worked as a porter at Guy's Hospital in London, as well as at the hospital in Newcastle.

I heard a lovely story about him recently. When he was dining in Trinity College one evening – on one of his rare appearances at High Table – there was a very creamy pudding for dessert. Wittgenstein began hesitantly to help himself, when a kind college servant bent over him and said softly in his ear, 'If you dig a little deeper, sir, you'll find a peach.' Wittgenstein said that was the kindest thing anyone ever said to him in all his years at Cambridge.

I offer that as a Thought for the Day, not least because it was not only what the great philosopher himself said, but what the servant said and did – the truth and importance of which the philosopher recognized.

'If you dig deeper, you'll find a peach.'

———————— •◆• ————————

87

Guy Fawkes' Day

Saturday 4 November 2000

Guy Fawkes' Day this year will be a very damp squib for thousands.
No good saying:

> Please to remember
> The fifth of November:
> Gunpowder treason and plot.
> I see no reason
> Why gunpowder treason
> Should ever be forgot

which almost every boy and girl was taught in my childhood. But a
lot has happened since then, besides this year's appalling floods. It
was, for instance, impossible to have bonfires after dark during the
war; and explosions then were rarely exciting or entertaining. We've
learnt that fireworks can be very dangerous. We've also learnt not to
be so romantic about Guy Fawkes' Day itself.

The plot to blow up Parliament, in 1605 was the product of
Catholic prejudice against Protestants – and vice versa. And in our
own day, in Northern Ireland, we've seen some of the tragic consequences of such prejudice. Thank God, the cause of Christian
Unity has advanced a good deal. And, thank God, most of us have
learnt that the best way to change a government is not by putting a
bomb under it but by the ballot box.

And yet I still look back with joy at the day when I was allowed
to hold my first sparkler in our back garden. And I still think we need
today a rebirth of wonder.

Of course, it's very possible to be superior when comparing
AD 2000 with AD 1600, and to forget that William Shakespeare and
George Herbert were alive and writing then.

And, in fact, the illustrious Dean of Westminster, Lancelot
Andrewes, was consecrated Bishop on the very day the Gunpowder
Plot was discovered, close by the Abbey. His book of private prayers

has much to teach us today, and so have his sermons, several of which he preached on the Gunpowder Plot itself.

Four years before that terrible event, Andrewes said in a sermon: 'God impeacheth not Caesar . . . In the high and heavenly work of the preservation of all our lives, persons, estates and goods in safety, peace and quietness – in this his so great and divine benefit he hath associated Caesar to himself.'

There's surely a Thought for the weekend of 'Gunpowder Treason and Plot' – and of the last days of the Presidential Election in the United States, and of crucial deliberations here on Petrol and Protest, and of planning to cope with the effect of the floods: that God has 'associated himself with the work of Caesar' – that's to say, the work of Government.

———— •◆• ————

88

Living with mystery

Saturday 30 December 2000

There are several mysteries in life which, with all our knowledge, and skill, and technical achievement, we've hardly begun to plumb.

I still think of Time as one of life's greatest mysteries. Of course, we can measure it – in minutes, and months, and millennia. We can 'tell the time'. We can save it, spend it and waste it. But no one knows when time began – or how it began, or when it will end. It's part of the raw material of our existence; and yet it's essentially a mystery.

But, as with other mysteries, because we can't always be facing the fact of our ignorance, we play a game of 'Let's pretend' – 'Let's pretend we know what Time it is', 'Let's forget the mystery of Time – for the time being.'

Yet it's dangerous to live as though we had solved a mystery when we haven't. It can turn us into 'know-alls', instead of being humble before the mysteries of life. Whatever else religion is, it's acknowledging and living with mystery.

A religious person, I'd say, is someone who consciously, daily, faces the mystery of life.

One of the reasons why Shakespeare is such a great playwright and poet is because he's always facing the mystery of Time, and is always facing his readers and hearers with that mystery. He has at least a hundred sayings on Time in his plays and poems. Sometimes he speaks quite angrily and resentfully of 'this bloody tyrant Time'. At other times he speaks wistfully: 'O Gentlemen,' says Hotspur, in *Henry IV*, 'the time of life is short".

We may not know precisely what was Shakespeare's religion, but we do know he was profoundly religious, and that he encourages us to be religious. He suggests in *King Lear* that we 'take upon's the mystery of things as if we were God's spies'.

And that we should surely do in the last hours of a year, and – as many would maintain – of a Millennium.

As 'God's spies' we can think of him creating Time, creating our life and times, our individual life and time, and the time that is the backcloth, so to speak, of the history of all humankind. And, as we step out into the unknown of a New Year, and a new Millennium, we can say with the Psalmist: 'My time is in thy hand.'

89

The journey

Saturday 6 January 2001

In all the great religions, the idea of pilgrimage has played an important part. Alongside it, there has often been the idea of the Spiritual Journey. Both these ideas meet, it seems to me, in the journey of the Wise Men to the manger at Bethlehem, which is celebrated by many today on this the Feast of the Epiphany. All this was the subject of one of the best-known poems of T. S. Eliot, which he published as a kind of 'pamphlet for Christmas'. It begins – very appropriately for this particular year – with these five lines:

> A cold coming we had of it,
> Just the worst time of the year
> For a journey, and such a long journey;
> The ways deep and the weather sharp,
> The very dead of winter.

What many people did not notice, was that those first five lines had quotation marks round them. Eliot had not written those lines himself; he had lifted them, unaltered, from a seventeenth-century sermon of Lancelot Andrewes. It had, in fact, been preached on Christmas Day 1622, before the Court of King James, when Andrewes was Dean of Westminster.

There's no doubt that Eliot thought the prose of Andrewes ranked with the finest English prose, not only of that time but of any time. He also reckoned Andrewes to be a superb preacher.

But it was not simply Andrewes' prose that had so greatly affected Eliot. It's not too much to say that Andrewes' sermon had affected Eliot's soul.

The Journey of the Magi is a poem about the painful necessity of rebirth for us all – which is itself a kind of journey from Death to Life – which Eliot felt he must describe in his poem in intensely personal terms. Peter Ackroyd, in his biography of Eliot, calls it 'the poem of a convert'. It's certainly a 'personal testimony' to a journey Eliot himself had made.

Today, on this Feast of the Epiphany, perhaps those first five lines of Eliot's poem may serve to remind us of that spiritual journey we all have to make – which is often quite painful – though

> 'Journey's End in Lover's meeting,
> Every Wise Man's son doth know.'

90

Problems into gifts

Saturday 13 January 2001

I was given two books for Christmas which at first sight seemed to be on separate subjects; but now I see them as having a lot to say to each other.

The first was called *Hitler's Gift*. It's about scientists who fled Nazi Germany. Twenty of them became Nobel prize-winners. Their stories are often gripping: stories of escape and rescue, but also, sometimes, of internment here, for a while, as enemy aliens.

When refugees arrive in a foreign country, there are always questions to be asked, now as then. But all the scientists, in the end, are able to say of Britain that what their country of adoption gave them was not just a new home and livelihood; they also found a new and better way of life. Of course, besides those scientists, there were thousands more refugees from Hitler with other gifts.

The second book is rather different. Its principal author is Mark Cutts, who works for the United Nations High Commission for Refugees. It's simply called *The State of the World's Refugees*, and sub-titled: *Fifty Years of Humanitarian Action*. Kofi Annan, the United Nations Secretary, has written the Preface. The first part of it is history: what's been done in the last 50 years about one of the most complex and major human problems of today. It looks closely at the challenge of the last ten years. And, with over a million people forced to flee their homes in Kosovo, East Timor, and Chechnya in 1999 – to say nothing of Africa or elsewhere – it's clear that the problem of asylum seekers will remain one of the major concerns of the international community in this twenty-first century.

So far, in Europe and North America, that concern has been expressed increasingly in more restrictive asylum policies.

Such a book on the state of the world's refugees will be a great help – not only in schools and universities, but to all of us who know this is an inescapable problem, and want to face some of its complexities.

But my two presents have taught me that seeing asylum seekers simply as a problem may be part of the problem. What struck me

125

about *Hitler's Gift* is that it never seems to be about a problem: it's about the harnessing and release of gifts.

Christians, in their prayers, often speak of meeting Christ in the stranger; but I do not myself believe that Christians have the monopoly of that attitude which greeted refugees from Hitler in, say, 1938, in such a way that turned them from being problems into gifts.

———————————•◆•———————————

91

Unity, peace and concord

Saturday 20 January 2001

Words – like most other things – have a life and death of their own. Take, for instance, the words: 'O God, who art the Author of Peace and Lover of Concord' – words I used every morning, 50 years ago, when I was first ordained – in what was surely one of the loveliest of prayers in the Prayer Book. But the first flight of Concorde ruined that prayer for good – or ill. You couldn't say it without thinking primarily of the plane. And then came the tragedy of Concorde. And, after that, all the intensive work to find out what precisely went wrong, and what would be needed to ensure that no such tragedy should ever occur again. And now, probably, it won't be long before Concorde is in regular flight again.

There is some benefit, I think, to the fact that we can never now use that prayer without having at the back of our minds the awful memory of tragedy, and an awareness of the cost – not just in cash, but in the efforts of the best brains – that has to be paid for there to be Concorde again. There will also be some who, when they think of Concorde, always think of possible damage to the environment.

In our new mental image of that word 'concord', there will undoubtedly be a new and painful realism

Many Americans – let it be said, this particular day – have never been able to use the word 'concord' without thinking, paradoxically, of the Battle of Concord, in Massachusetts, in 1775, in which British soldiers clashed with American militiamen.

It seems to me that when we pray for 'unity, peace and concord' – as many will no doubt be doing this Week of Prayer for Christian Unity – we should be aware of the cost and effort that must inevitably accompany that prayer, it if be real and genuine; and that in this world we shall never be beyond tragedy.

Many years ago, I was best man to a fellow curate in Westminster, who was a Canadian, as was his bride. He became a bishop in Canada, and has only recently retired. His future mother-in-law said to me – with great vigour and passion – as we stood waiting for the photographer to complete his work on that wedding day: 'Eric, always remember: marriages have to be worked at!'

I've never forgotten her words. And, this morning, I would only add: 'And so, too, does unity, peace and concord' – among nations, families, friends and churches.

———— •◆• ————

92

Where can I best serve?

Saturday 24 February 2001

I never quite know what to make of St Matthias whose saint's day it is today. He was chosen as an apostle, in place of Judas Iscariot; but there's no mention of him other than when he was chosen; and that happened in the oddest way. They prayed; then they drew lots, gambled; and of the two candidates, Matthias was the winner.

Well, we've learnt only this year that electing even presidents can be a bit of a lottery – and maybe we shall have more to learn when our own election comes. But choosing apostles – and ministers of religion in general – you rather hope, and expect, to involve, let's say, more than 'providential accident'.

Recently, a friend of mine, who's been both a parish priest and a director of social services for a whole county, made a passionate appeal for people to consider offering themselves for training to fill the many vacancies there are now in child care and child protection teams, and in other posts in the social services; in the teaching profession; in the police and prison service; and the health service.

On St Matthias' Day, I want to suggest that the question 'How can I best serve God and the world?' is one of the most important questions that every human being has to ask and answer – and to go on asking and answering. But I don't pretend this is always an entirety rational process.

I remember once sitting in a train when a complete stranger entered the carriage and sat opposite me, and I was overwhelmed by the conviction that I must say to him: 'You'll never be happy 'til you're ordained.' Eventually, I summoned up the courage to say just that to him – and blurted it out. To my surprise, he answered quietly: 'I know, but I've just signed up for three years for a job in Africa.' Over ten years later, I met him again, by chance, in Sri Lanka. He had, by then, been trained for ordination, and was already serving there as a priest.

That's not the way people usually discover what they're meant to do in life – no more than is drawing lots.

But what's important, whatever our age, is to go on asking the question, and pressing it: 'Where can I now best serve God and the world?' That may mean some form of selection, and some further training – and, sometimes, there's the financing of the training to be faced. But the question, 'Where can I best serve?' is of continuing and over-riding importance.

And, like Matthias, we may be surprised how we're enabled and equipped to do a necessary and worthwhile job.

———— •◆• ————

93

My God, my God, why?

Saturday 3 March 2001

On 19 March 1866, the Revd Canon Sir James Erasmus Phillips, Baronet, vicar of the small market town of Warminster in Wiltshire, wrote a letter to his parishioners from the piazza in Rome, where he was staying on holiday. He said:

> I was so thankful to hear that the Days of Humiliation for the Cattle Plague were so well observed in Warminster. May we all own this chastisement as a loud call to us to mend our lives and to walk more closely with our God.

No one can imagine a vicar today writing like that to his people. We have, alas the Cattle Plague today – and call it, of course, foot and mouth disease; but no one would proclaim it a chastisement from God, nor would anyone call for 'Days of Humiliation' in response to such an outbreak.

It would do us all good, I think, to contemplate the change that has happened in about 150 years, and to evaluate it as best we can – and to think what it has to say to us for the future.

We might do this for several reasons.

We might do it as an act of sympathy for the farmers and others who are suffering such 'Days of Humiliation' – which may turn into weeks and months – because of the present outbreak of foot and mouth disease.

We might do it for our own sake and our children's sake; for all of us need to ask and answer the question where we think God is in all this: and thereby, who we think God is. We all need to face again, from time to time, whether there's any meaning at all within all this chaos, a sense of chaos to which this week's freak but tragic rail accident has, alas, contributed.

It will be easy for some simply to say, with no regret: 'God is dead!' Others will not believe this to be true, though they may not be able to express why they hang on to belief in God. It's my own experience that my faith has often grown and become most strong

129

when, for instance, I have had before me – as I did quite recently – a friend's dead child, or when I've been faced with the collapse of some project in which I've put a great deal of hope and trust. It's then that I've found myself putting my trust afresh in the God who, I believe, revealed himself most clearly in a man at the end of his tether, who cried out – with those other human beings who've lost everything: 'My God, my God, why hast Thou forsaken me?' – and just 'hung in there', as we say, on a cross.

94

Humour in heaven

Saturday 10 March 2001

Two of my friends, Sybil and Helen – both in their nineties – have died this week. When I was a curate in Westminster 50 years ago, I prepared Helen for Confirmation. Her funeral takes place today. I can never forget her Confirmation. She was in mid-life, and was suffering from a nervous illness at the time, and could not face large public occasions. But a family friend, then Bishop of Norwich, said he'd come and confirm her privately, with just a few people gathered in the side-chapel of our church.

It so happened that, at that time, the church boiler was being repaired immediately below the chapel. We decided there was no need to interrupt the workmen. But it meant that, at the very moment the bishop laid his hands on Helen's head, and said that lovely prayer: 'Defend, O Lord, this child with thy heavenly grace, that she may continue thine for ever . . .' a workman dropped a heavy pipe on his foot, and let out what I will call a well-known Cockney expletive, which he addressed directly to the Almighty. The words clearly ascended to us above, through a heating grill. The kneeling vicar, George Reindorp, and the clutch of assistant clergy kneeling alongside him, somehow managed to contain themselves.

In the vestry after the service, the Bishop, gaitered in those days – and a fine figure of a man – simply said, with a smile: 'Wasn't it good that the prayers of those below us should be united with our prayers for Helen?'

It was, as I say, a most memorable service. But it was not least its humour which made it so memorable. When I come to put down on paper why I believe in God, I find I always have to include humour. It's such a uniquely human gift. I've looked everywhere for a good definition of it, but have never found one completely satisfying. And yet we all know what it is – and know it above all when it's absent.

Mark Twain said categorically, as if he had particular reason to know: 'There is no humour in heaven.' I beg to differ. I believe that the God who created us with a sense of humour will have prepared for us in heaven new and unexpected ways of revealing it. Heaven without humour won't be heaven!

Of course, there's a time to be humorous and a time not to be. That's why I think heaven will be the time and the place for it. Helen and Sybil will certainly both appreciate it. But they won't be alone.

———— •◆• ————

95

Almighty God . . .

Saturday 17 March 2001

For nearly 50 years, I've had a fellow feeling for Eliza Doolittle, if you'll forgive that sexist phrase. In *My Fair Lady* – which derives, of course, from Shaw's *Pygmalion*, and which has just been revived at the National Theatre – Eliza has to submit herself to an expert speech trainer, in order to be delivered from her Cockney accent.

Well, the first week I was ordained, in 1951, to a curacy in Westminster, my vicar, George Reindorp, summoned me to his study, and said: 'I'm afraid I must send you to a speech therapist. We must get rid of your Cockney accent.' I swallowed hard. I'd been to school in Dagenham, and was proud of it. My new boss clearly knew what he was talking about. He was well known for doing what was called *Lift Up Your Hearts* on the BBC of a morning – the predecessor of *Thought for the Day*. My duty, as a fledgling priest, was – it seemed – to pocket my pride.

When I went along to my 'Professor Higgins', I must admit I felt I was going to have my backbone removed. But, as things turned out, I learnt more from him than I could ever have dared imagine. For six months, he only asked me to say what's called, in the Prayer Book, 'The Collect for Purity', which begins: 'Almighty God, unto whom all hearts be open, all desires known, and from whom no secrets are hid . . .' In fact, in the first weeks he only wanted me to say the very first words. He said: 'You know, you're not thinking what you're saying. You're not thinking of "Almighty God". You're just reading without thinking. I want you to be silent for a while and think of "Almighty God" – and then try and say those two words in a way that conveys what you have in mind, who you have in mind.' And he said: 'You know, your job as a priest is a terrifying one. You've not only got to say what the words mean to you, you've got to say them in such a way that those who hear you will catch at least a glimpse of who you have in mind.'

The odd thing is that Mr Medlicott (that was the name of my 'Professor Higgins') taught me more about prayer and worship, and how to conduct it, than any of my mentors. He never mentioned my Cockney accent. And I still don't know whether I had one or lost one. It didn't seem to matter. But, for better, for worse, here I am now on the BBC, talking about 'Almighty God – to whom all hearts are open, all desires known, and from whom no secrets are hid.'

———— •◆• ————

96

Withdrawal with intent to return

Saturday 28 July 2001

This weekend is the busiest weekend at airports, with people flying off on holiday. Certainly all this week I seem to have been talking to people who were just about to go away – teachers who were glad that, at last, term was over; children who were excited about where they were off to.

They've reminded me just how much holidays meant to me when I was a child. It was only a week on the south or east coast then, and I remember how bitterly disappointed we all were one year, during the Depression, in the Thirties, when all thought of a holiday had to be abandoned.

Years later, just after the Second World War, I happened to be reading, as a student, a remarkable book by Arnold Toynbee called *A Study of History*, in which the author drew attention to the huge contribution made to the history of civilizations by individuals and sometimes small groups, because they had discovered what he called 'the principle of "withdrawal with intent to return"'. He said that through such withdrawal for a time, people and societies often realized powers within themselves which might otherwise have remained dormant. He saw this time of withdrawal as an opportunity – and, perhaps, a necessary condition – for the transformation of whole societies.

It's interesting that in the ministry of Jesus we can see clearly this rhythm of 'withdrawal and return'. Before each significant stage in his revelation of himself to his disciples, Jesus withdrew himself. He was 'moved with compassion for the multitudes' because they were as 'sheep not having a shepherd'; because they were hungry and needy. Yet, often, in the midst of all that need, we're told simply: 'He withdrew himself.'

It's an aspect of the life of Jesus to which, perhaps, too little attention has been given. Yet maybe it has something important to say, not only to the Church but to the world at large.

Unless I'm much mistaken, there's a confusion about our world today. Many individuals and societies seem to be caught up in a kind of chaotic and mindless busy-ness. Maybe those five words 'Withdrawal with intent to return' have a message for us. In a way, they describe what we want when we go off on holiday. But the danger today is that our holidays may be just as busy and frenetic as our working life. Unconsciously they're a recognition – a wistful recognition, maybe – of the profound need at the heart of our lives. But that unconscious need has somehow to be brought to the surface.

We all need consciously to seek 'withdrawal with intent to return'.

97

Ageing – and the Queen Mother

Saturday 4 August 2001

Ageing is a curious phenomenon which we all have to face.

Last year, when I was 75, I put on my wall a text from St John's gospel – 'Thou hast kept the good wine until now' – just to remind myself never to think that all the good things happen when we're young. But I did it also because, at that time, I'd had to take the funerals of several of my friends and contemporaries. And watching your friends leave this world ahead of you is one of the most taxing characteristics of growing old

I've found myself this last week – not least as a Chaplain to the Queen – asking myself what I would say to someone who was having to go into hospital when she was 100, and who must be only too aware of what soon lies ahead of her – as it does, in due course, for us all.

In fact, I don't suppose the Queen Mother would need anyone to remind her of what her husband said, so movingly, in his Christmas broadcast of 1939: 'Put your hand into the hand of God. That shall be better to you than light, and safer than a known way.'

The Queen Mother has displayed throughout her life an infectious courage, not least through her smile. Sometimes it's difficult to believe that she has been a widow for half her life. Her birthday today will bring back many memories of her cheerfulness.

I particularly remember her visit, in the 1980s, to a church in South London – St Peter's, Walworth, near the East Street market. Just as she was setting out for the church, she was told that all the lights in the church had failed. She arrived with a torch and told the vicar they had a tool bag in the back of the car if he needed it. 'But I'm sure you've got plenty of candles!' she added with a smile.

In the vicarage, after the service, she discussed with the vicar the problems of the large high-rise flats on a new estate near the church. When she went down into the crypt below the church, where the people met to drink and dance and sing, she particularly wanted to meet anyone who was as old as she was.

Many will want to say a heartfelt 'Happy Birthday' to the Queen Mother today. Maybe the memories of the powerful contribution she made, not only to her own family but to life in Britain today, can remind us of what the elderly, not least grandparents, have to give to life.

But maybe it can also bring to our minds, by contrast, the elderly who are not in the public eye; indeed, who, in the nature of things, have to spend much time alone. For the reality is that ageing and loneliness all too often go together. And the care of the elderly is surely one of the chief hallmarks of a caring society.

———— ◆ ————

98

Faith and music

Saturday 11 August 2001

The recent deaths of Larry Adler, and of Joseph Cooper, of *Face the Music* fame – and, indeed, this evening's broadcast on BBC Television of the Promenade Concert, creating a huge audience – all serve to remind us what music-makers and music-lovers we human beings are. For me, as for many, music lies near the heart of my religion.

There are, I think, several reasons why faith and music go together. Anyone who's attended a performance of, say, a Beethoven sonata by a great pianist, will know that they've been present at a marvellous act of creation – by the pianist, but also by the composer. But when music reveals our human gifts of creation, it's a sort of spy hole on all our creative powers – as artists, gardeners, cooks. Religion and creation go together.

But music has even more to offer us. It provides us with another language – to interpret our human experience and the mystery of life itself: its pain and its joy; its good and its evil. Where words fail, music often succeeds.

And then there's the beauty of music. Every experience of beauty in this world is a kind of breakthrough to another world than this: an echo of an eternal harmony. I would go so far as to say that each experience of beauty is the call of God; and music is one of the ways in which we hear and respond to that call.

It's paradoxical that music is always so down-to-earth. It involves the use of our bodies, to make sounds as singers or as instrumentalists. But although it begins with things like five-finger exercises, it helps us to get to heaven. It enables us to know just what a single body can achieve as, say, a singer or as people together in a choir or an orchestra. It gives us a vision of what we were meant to be or do, both individually and together.

And then there's music and time. Every musician understands something of the mystery of time. Rhythm is to do with time. Time is essential to music. Yet, often, by employing time, it gives us a vision of what lies beyond time. Time did not intimidate a composer like Johann Sebastian Bach. He employed it to the glory of God. And he even employed silence, rests, in achieving his purpose.

Edward Elgar set to matchless music the words of the Irish poet Arthur O'Shaughnessy:

> We are the music makers
> And we are the dreamers of dreams.

———◆◆———

99

Fellow delinquents

Saturday 18 August 2001

Just before Robert Runcie retired as Archbishop of Canterbury, he asked me to join the group of people called 'Archbishop's Advisers', who look after clergy who have been found guilty of some serious offence – probably involving alcohol, money or sex. My first instinct was to refuse, but Robert Runcie said: 'I've never given you an order before, and I can't now; but I very much hope you will take on this work – I think it's so important.' So I did what I was asked, and have now been doing it for ten years.

The people I have to see, are, mercifully, few in number. Sometimes they're angry with the Church; and, of course, sometimes people are angry with them – parishioners, colleagues, bishops and, above all, understandably, their victims.

Sometimes they're quite relieved that they've been found out – after maybe many years of unsuccessfully struggling with their particular temptation. Sometimes they don't accept the reality of what has happened, and their part in it, and try to blame others. Sometimes they're dismayed, depressed and disgusted with themselves at what's happened.

Sometimes there's been a split in them. They've split off their professional and priestly self from the realities of their personal self; and if they're to be redeemed and restored they have to be helped to

137

come to terms with that reality, though restoration to office is not possible after some offences.

Sometimes my job is to find a good psychotherapist for the priest. Sometimes it means finding the funds that that kind of help requires. Always it's my job to help the priest come to terms with reality, which includes, of course, the reality of the continuing healing power of the love of God.

What saddens me is that, often, the discovery of a delinquent priest is greeted with barely concealed pleasure on the part of the press. Then the sin of the priest is compounded by the sin of the press.

I'm now very thankful that Robert Runcie pressed me to take on this particular task. It's a huge privilege. It has underlined for me, if it needed underlining, that whatever priests are, they never cease to be human. I carefully call those I look after 'my fellow delinquent priests', because it's reminded me that in every human being – male and female, ordained and lay – there's a spoilt priest; and we all need to be loved back into life and wholeness and ministry.

———— •◆• ————

100

God Save the Queen

Saturday 1 June 2002

It was in 1984 that I was first told that the Queen was minded to make me one of her Chaplains.

The bishop who told me said it was more in the nature of an enquiry as to how I would respond to such an invitation.

I found myself thinking immediately of some of my ecclesiastical heroes who had accepted a royal appointment, such as the much-loved East End socialist priest, Fr John Groser.

Then I started to think out just why I believed in the monarchy, and what it meant when I said, and sang, 'God *Save* the Queen'.

I reminded myself first what Robert Runcie, then Archbishop of Canterbury, had said, in July 1980, on the Queen Mother's eightieth birthday: 'Royalty puts a human face on the operation of government.'

Then I found myself thinking about symbolism.

As a priest, I have for years been involved in the world of symbols – bread and wine, and dog-collars!, and priesthood itself. And, clearly, the symbolism of monarchy is also hugely important.

Symbols, it seems to me, are different from signals – like red and green traffic lights. Symbols are part of the language which enables us human beings to express our history and our historical identity with our fellow human beings, our belonging to a particular human community. They play a profound part in integrating and unifying human beings – and act powerfully at the conscious and unconscious levels.

Clearly, that's true of the regalia of royalty: the crown, for instance, and the coronation, the anointing, the sceptre, the orb with the cross set over it, can only be understood by taking their symbolism seriously. And one thing is absolutely sure – the Queen herself has taken that symbolism *very* seriously. Indeed, the Queen has taken her calling to be the Queen as seriously as any priests I've ever known have taken their ordination.

Her coronation the Queen understood to be her ordination to her calling to serve.

In September, I hope to be celebrating the fiftieth anniversary of my ordination; so I understand a little just how the Queen must be feeling about the fiftieth anniversary of her coronation. And I feel thankful and privileged to have been – for nearly twenty years now – Chaplain to a Queen who has lived out her vocation with such commitment and selfless devotion.

I'm very glad I said 'Yes' to the Queen's invitation; and I find myself saying today, as I expect most of you do, a sincere and heart-felt 'God save – God preserve, sustain and bless – the Queen.'